Branding

2nd edition

A PRACTICAL GUIDE TO PLANNING YOUR STRATEGY

GEOFFREY RANDALL

IN ASSOCIATION WITH

Marketing MAGAZINE

KOGAN
PAGE

First published in 1997
Reprinted 1998
Second edition 2000

Kogan Page Limited
120 Pentonville Road
London
N1 9JN
UK

Kogan Page Limited
163 Central Avenue, Suite 2
Dover
NH 03820
USA

British Library Cataloguing in Publication Data

A CIP record for this book is available from the British Library.

ISBN 0 7494 32810

Typeset by Jean Cussons Typesetting, Diss, Norfolk
Printed and bound in Great Britain by Clays Ltd, St Ives plc

Contents

Preface to the Second Edition

The first edition of this small book was published in 1997 and, as it sold gratifyingly well, was rapidly reprinted with minor corrections. However, as the world appears to be moving ever faster, by 1999 it seemed that a new edition was needed.

The major change has, of course, been the extraordinary development of the Internet during this time, in particular the growth of commercial applications of the World Wide Web. It seems impossible now that Netscape was registered as a company only in 1995, and the few years since then have seen its dramatic rise, mid-life struggles and eventual takeover by America Online (AOL). The fact that in early 2000 AOL had a stock market valuation double that of Time Warner, and was able to announce an agreed merger with – really a takeover of – that media giant, underlines the speed and ramifications of the changes.

This second edition, therefore, includes a new chapter devoted to the Internet and its implications for brands and branding. This is the major addition, but I have also taken the opportunity to update other material and add examples to it. Some details will still be out of date by the time you read this book, but I believe that the basic principles it outlines will remain true whatever happens over the next few years.

Geoffrey Randall
January 2000

1

What is a Brand?

'NO ONE EVER GOT FIRED FOR BUYING IBM'

What a wonderful testament to the power of a brand. This saying used to be common in the computer business, in the days when IBM (International Business Machines) dominated the world market in a way in which few companies have ever dominated any one field – with 60 per cent of sales and up to 80 per cent of world profits. From IBM's story we can draw many lessons that will help us in trying to define exactly what it is that separates a brand from a mere product.

Decisions to buy IBM equipment were made by hard-nosed, analytical business people, and those decisions were often about purchases amounting to millions of US dollars for products that might be fundamental to the buyer's operations. This is a business-to-business market, and one in which decisions are supposedly based on rational, unemotional calculations. Yet in this case, customers were buying the *brand*. IBM machines were rarely the most technologically advanced, and were almost never the cheapest.

What IBM had created was a total offering of hardware, software and services – this gave buyers a set of benefits that no competitor could match. The benefits which customers were buying included confidence in the quality and reliability of the equipment and the longevity of the supplier. They bought business solutions – not technical specifications – and they felt complete confidence in IBM.

More recently, however, IBM lost touch with developments in their industry and very nearly gave away the priceless advantage that their brand building had given them. They allowed new competitors to steal market share – and they let Microsoft take over the dominating position in the industry. We can see, then, that although a strong brand can confer enormous power, it is not eternal or immune from attack. It must be carefully built, and maintained with fierce commitment and unwavering focus.

As we all live surrounded by brands, it may seem idle to spend time on defining them. We are all familiar with leading brands such as Persil, Guinness, Mars, Sony, and Coca-Cola. We could all name brands we grew up with, and perhaps still use. We could nominate favourite brands – those we feel we can rely on, those we treat as old friends. We could all probably come up with a reasonable shot at a definition of a brand: it would probably contain words such as 'unique', 'name', 'identity', 'differentiation', 'quality' and 'guarantee'. Why do we need to elaborate further?

The argument of this book is that brands are so fundamentally important to the survival and success of many firms that we need to understand them in all their subtleties and complexities *so that we can manage them correctly*. Strong brands are powerful and profitable, but there are many challenges and threats to their continuing strength and even their existence. Unless we can tease out the true meaning of a brand, we cannot hope to identify and meet these challenges.

Indeed, management consultants McKinsey have argued that companies will need to win *the right to brand*. Briefly, they claim the company that wins the right to brand in a given market will need to meet three criteria: 1) it is part of a winning value proposition; 2) it controls the core assets to deliver the value; and 3) it owns the consumer relationship in the most efficient way (Freeling, 1994).

This reminds us of some key issues in branding – issues that underlie much of what follows but are easy to forget:

■ Branding is a fundamental *strategic* process that involves all parts of the firm in its delivery. It is about marketing, but is not confined to the marketing department.
■ The brand must always deliver *value*, and the value must be defined in *consumer* terms.

■ The brand has a continuing *relationship* with its buyers and users; this may change over time, but the firm must always work to maintain it.

■ Because competition is getting fiercer all the time, and because structural changes undermine the status quo, branding must be *continuously adapted* so that it is both effective and efficient.

Let us therefore explore first what brands are.

CHARACTERISTICS OF BRANDS

'Brands are a part of the fabric of life.'   (David Ogilvy)

'Just about the only thing brands have in common is a kind of fame.'
(Jeremy Bullmore)

These two quotations, from two famous British advertising men of different generations, seem contradictory. McDonald's is part of life, but is it famous in the way Clint Eastwood is? Porsche is famous, but is it part of our lives?

Judie Lannon, another advertising person, relates anthropological findings on cult and ritual to some brands: *'The brand is a cult object… it has charisma.'* One can see the connection for brands she quotes such as Zippo lighters, Swatch watches or Mont Blanc pens. Perhaps it works also for more mundane brands such as Domestos, and may throw light on any brand if we look deeply enough.

An allied view is of 'the brand as hero'. Again, we can see this more easily for some brands than others. Heroic imagery is part of some brand advertising; this is obvious in the case of Marlboro cigarettes, where cigarette smoking can have overtones of rugged independence and individualism. It is less obvious what overt heroism has to do with chocolates, except that perhaps the lady who loves Milk Tray also loves heroes. Today, the hero is often female, as in advertising for Volkswagen and Nissan cars.

This leads us to ask, which is the hero – the brand or the user? In much British advertising, gentle humour disguises but does not conceal the hero. If heavy beer drinkers are hero-worshipping fantasists, as one study suggested, then much advertising is well targeted ('I bet he drinks Carling Black Label').

What these views all suggest is that a *brand* must be something different from a *product*. Arguably, all brands start as undifferentiated products; their success or failure in the market place depends on their functional quality. When soap came in large blocks from which your grocer cut off a slice when you asked for it, you judged it as soap. After Sunlight started to wrap uniform blocks in recognizable packaging, you could begin to differentiate the Sunlight brand from ordinary soap as a product. When Virgin first started, it sold music as a product. Gradually, the Virgin *brand* was built up and now covers an astonishing array of product fields including airlines, cola, railways and financial services. Virgin is now quite definitely a brand, something different from any of its individual products. (We shall return later to the issue of brand extension and the Virgin phenomenon.)

A *brand*, then, has an existence that is more than an actual product or service: it has a life of its own that feeds on the original product, but can also carry its values and identity into new product areas.

As Stephen King put it, 'A product is something that is made in a factory; a brand is something that is bought by a consumer' (1990). Charles Revson, the founder of Revlon, made a similar point when he said that in the factory, he made cosmetics; in the store, his customers bought hope. 'Thomas Cook' means something to us; it carries with it associations and memories that are generically to do with travel (and perhaps with tradition and reliability), but which are not necessarily tied exclusively to shops or traveller's cheques. If electronic technology completely replaces existing cameras and film, Kodak could still be a leading brand, though one that represents excellence in image capture, storage and reproduction. Marks & Spencer can sell us financial services that have very little to do with its core business, because we have enormous trust in it as a brand. The brand, then, is a holistic combination of product and added values. As Jeremy Bullmore has pointed out:

> It is in every human being's nature to invent and build brand values inside each individual head. We do it with people, we do it with animals – and we do it with inanimate objects. The skill of brand management is to see that each consumer is offered the right raw materials from which he or she will build the brand as the brand owner would prefer. A brand is not an objective fact; it is made up of

a million or more individual and subjective assessments – a consensus of subjectivity.

(Bullmore, 1999)

Brands can exist in any field. Most of the examples given, and most well-known brands, are from the fast-moving consumer goods (fmcg) area, but we can also think of McDonald's, Singapore Airlines, Club Med, Holiday Inn, Disney, JCB, Caterpillar, the Prudential and many more. Later chapters will examine the issues of business-to-business and services branding in more detail, but examples from these fields will continue to crop up in our discussion here.

The very variety of the range of brands means that any single definition is likely to be either too limiting or very unwieldy. Some experts have even categorized brand definitions under six headings:

1. visual;
2. perceptual;
3. positioning;
4. added value;
5. image; and
6. personality (Hankinson and Cowking, 1993).

This gives an idea of the kinds of definitions available and the dimensions analysts use. No one definition will be adopted here, especially as there is not only a very wide range of brands, but also a range of types or levels of brand. This may seem to beg the question posed at the beginning of the section, but one study also found that leading consultants are not willing to limit themselves to a single definition (de Chernatony and Riley, 1996). Is there some litmus test that we can apply which will tell us infallibly whether something is a product or a brand? Is there a magic moment at which the beautiful brand butterfly emerges from the larva of a mere product?

It is rather like the difference between poetry and verse. Many people would say that they recognize 'real poetry' when they see it, but they could not produce an unambiguous definition of it. Different people will have differing views about certain works – some claiming that Kipling, for example, wrote poetry (even if 'good bad poetry'), while others maintain that he wrote nothing but verse.

The analogy with brands and products is that it is at the border between the two that disagreement is possible. Everyone agrees that Coca-Cola, Mars, Persil and so on are brands. The problem arises with newer or less well-established entities. It has been argued that Virgin is not a brand, because it depends almost entirely on the publicity generated by Richard Branson. Others have said that the Prudential, for example, is not a brand. My own view would be the opposite in both cases. The test must surely lie, not in the views of individual commentators, but in the collective opinion of the target customers and consumers. If they can perceive that a product has a unique identity that differentiates it from other similar products, and they can describe it and the unique set of benefits it offers, then it is a brand.

Certainly it is not the manufacturer or supplier who decides whether it is a brand or not. Some attempts to create brands – by British clearing banks, for instance – have manifestly not succeeded. To an outsider, the failure seems to have been due to their inability to persuade consumers that what they were offering really was unique and different. It is likely that at the time, the reality of bank services had not changed very much, and that of course was how consumers perceived matters. The 'branding' was just an expensive advertising campaign, making claims that no one believed. This underlines the point made at the beginning of the chapter, that branding is a matter for the whole firm, not just for the marketing department – particularly a weak and semi-detached marketing department with no real influence on the firm's products and services.

What we can conclude is that there are strong, successful brands at one end of a spectrum; at the other end are failed attempts at branding, where consumers perceive no unique characteristics distinguishing the product from others; and in between are brands of varying strengths and weaknesses. To analyse them more fully, we need to look at the dimensions that describe brands.

DIMENSIONS OF BRANDS

As suggested earlier, there are many models of brands. There is no one correct model that everyone accepts – as is so often the case in marketing. Here we will look at two which are representative. First, let us distinguish between brand image and brand identity.

Brand image is a phrase used rather loosely, particularly by people outside marketing – 'Let's change the image', they say hopefully of a brand in trouble. In fact, the image of a brand is what exists *in the minds of consumers*. It is *the total of all the information they have received about the brand* – from experience, word of mouth, advertising, packaging, service and so on – modified by selective perception, previous beliefs, social norms and forgetting. It may be messy and untidy, not what we would prefer; but it is what exists, and what we must work on and from.

Brand identity is what we transmit to the market place – it is what is under our control, provided that we understand the essence and expression of our brand. It is here that models can be useful. One model, shown in Figure 1.1, is from the Leo Burnett Brand Consultancy, and uses the dimensions: functions; personality/image; source; and differences.

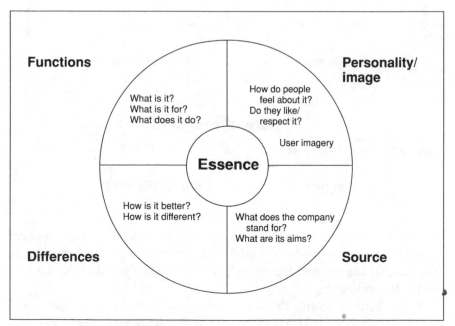

Source: Leo Burnett Brand Consultancy

Figure 1.1 *Burnett model of brand dimensions*

The dimensions form the brand's 'essence' at the centre. Brand identity will be strong when there is consistency between the dimensions, and they are supporting each other. If any dimension is weak or sending conflicting messages, then the resulting image in consumers' minds will be confused.

A second model, shown in Figure 1.2, is from Kapferer (1992). His dimensions are: physique; personality; culture; relationship; reflection; and self-image.

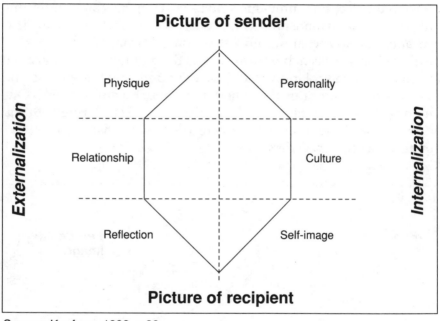

Source: Kapferer, 1992, p 38

Figure 1.2 *Kapferer's prism of identity*

By *physique* Kapferer means what others refer to as 'function', and is wider than the mere physical characteristics of the brand. It is the central purpose of the brand, the 'What does it do?' of the Leo Burnett model.

Personality is straightforward, and has been widely used as a main dimension in fmcg markets for decades. Consumers can describe brands' personalities, and are asked to do so through the sort of projective techniques described in Chapter 4.

Culture can belong either to the brand itself or to the parent company. Mercedes Benz cars have a strong cultural dimension: in their world, engineering excellence and solidity rank high, whereas more modish ideas about styling and features are seen as fripperies. Nike projects a culture of individual effort and commitment to success.

Because in most product markets people buy repeatedly, they can have *relationships* with brands over time. This is an important idea, since many views of markets seem to be based on a view that they are made up of unrelated transactions. While the move from transaction to relationship is most often talked about in fields like banking, it is found in most markets. It is clear that establishing a relationship between brand and user is healthy and positive – provided that the relationship is itself positive.

By *reflection* we mean the type of user that the brand appears to be aimed at. This is not necessarily the same as the brand's target market as described in its marketing plan, since many reflections are aspirational: they show the sort of person that the user would like to be, or aspires to be like. Most women know that they do not look like the photographs in cosmetic advertising, but they would prefer to be more like them. Men buying Marlboro cigarettes are not going to be cowboys, but would like to think of themselves as sharing some of the figure's characteristics.

The *self-image* is the internal version of the reflection. We are familiar with the idea that we are what we eat, and perhaps also with the idea that we are what we buy. The brands we buy represent, at least to some extent, our view of ourselves. Even someone who rejects brands by buying own label is saying something: 'I am the sort of person who is rational and buys on value for money, not meaningless advertising.'

To repeat, a strong brand is one that has a *consistent, coherent identity*. There is interaction between the different dimensions, and the company must work out what the detailed identity of the brand is, ensure that it is coherent across all the dimensions, and communicate it to the target audience.

LEVELS AND TYPES OF BRAND

Branding can be applied at different levels of the firm. Unfortunately, there is little agreement about the exact terms to be used for the levels, and there can be some confusion – particularly around such words as 'umbrella' or 'pillar' brands. There can also be overlap between categories – for example, between product brands and line brands – or changes over time in the way a brand name is used. What matters is the extent to which a particular analysis helps our understanding of a particular situation, but remember that different people may mean different things by the same word.

Product brands or *stand-alone brands*. In its basic form, the brand is identical with a single product or service – Mars bars, for example. Many leading companies use this approach; there is no Procter and Gamble brand, even though Procter and Gamble is probably the leading branding company in the world. Its brands are all individually named – Ariel, Fairy, Crest, Pampers. There may of course be sub-products of each brand, such as Boy and Girl Pampers, or different types of toothpaste.

Line brands. Here a group of products are given a name, such as 'L'Oréal StudioLine'. All the products in the line will be in a similar field, and will be positioned at the same quality/value level.

Range brands. A slightly wider grouping may be called a range, though it must be said that this is a subjective decision. Weight Watchers from Heinz is a range, but whether Vidal Sassoon (from Procter and Gamble) is a line or a range is an open question.

Umbrella and *pillar brands*. An umbrella, as the name suggests, gives protection to several sub-brands. One example, called pillar branding by its owners Birds Eye Foods, is shown in Figure 1.3.

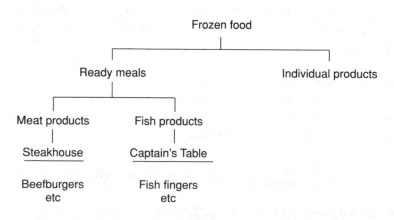

Figure 1.3 *An example of pillar branding used by Birds Eye*

Umbrella branding is used by other commentators to refer to what we have termed line or range brands, or to the next level up when a company name identifies the brand.

Company, family or *source brands*. Examples of this are common: Sony, Ford, IBM and Cadbury.

Endorsing company, corporate or *banner brands*. Here the company name appears, but less prominently than the main brand; it acts as an endorsement or guarantee. An example is the brand KitKat, with Nestlé as the endorsing company (formerly, of course, the endorsing company was Rowntree). The level of identification and endorsement varies from prominent to understated.

Not only are there different levels of brand, there are also various types of brand. There are *designer labels* such as Armani or Porsche Design. There are *griffes*, or *haute couture brands*: *griffe*, apart from meaning 'claw', also refers to the signature and thence the brand of fashion houses such as Christian Dior. There is clearly some overlap with designer labels. *Licensed names are another type of brand*, of which Disney is the best-known example. Finally, there are *retailers' brands*. In fmcg markets, these are the most important; they include store name brands, lines or sub-brands, and generics; they will be discussed in more detail in Chapter 7.

Out there in the real world, there is a mixture of styles of branding. The questions we should ask ourselves are 'What are we communicating to our target customers and consumers?' and 'What is the best way of communicating what we want to?'

To the obvious question 'What is the best way of doing it?' there is unfortunately – but unsurprisingly – no answer. Kellogg's brands all its products with the company name; Procter and Gamble uses stand-alone brands. Both were, until recently, supremely successful. It may be argued that the range of Procter and Gamble's products is much broader – and therefore it makes less sense to try to impose a single brand – whereas Kellogg's produces only breakfast cereals, and even Nestlé, with a huge number of products, is still a food company. There is a discernible trend towards the use of the company name. (This important topic will be dealt with at greater length in Chapter 10.)

We will now continue our exploration of branding by looking at the functions carried out by brands.

WHAT DO BRANDS DO?

If we ask what brands do for customers and consumers, one answer (adapted from Randall, 1993) is that they perform five main functions:

■ Identity: the brand must identify itself clearly and unambiguously, so name, legal protection and design elements are important.

■ Shorthand summary: the identity should act as a summary of all the information the consumer holds about the brand. Memory seems to work by storing packets of information in networks, and the brand should provide access to this network, triggering associations.

■ Security: buying a familiar brand should be reassuring. The brand should guarantee to provide the benefits expected.

■ Differentiation: the brand must clearly differentiate itself from its competitors, and show buyers how it is unique.

■ Added value: the brand must offer more than the generic product.

All great brands give you these benefits. Think about any of the brands you buy, and see how they work for you. In different situations, the elements may vary in importance, but they should all be there. Security may be of enormous value where there is a high level of uncertainty or risk (buying a computer system), added value more important when the actual difference between competing products is superficially small (shampoo). Exactly how the firm delivers the benefits will also vary: they may use superior technology, lower cost, strength in distribution, history or creative advertising. The brand will certainly need to harness the strength of the company as a whole in order to succeed over a long period.

Another view is that brands need to excel in offering at least one of the three key benefits: 1) price (such as Asda); 2) functional benefit (such as Toyota); or 3) psychological benefit (such as Timotei) (Davidson, 1997). While this view has the virtue of simplicity, it does not recognize the fact that many brands offer more than one benefit. Indeed, it could be argued that in most of today's highly competitive markets, a level of functionality is taken for granted and the general price level is also dictated by competition. Brands will then be trying – sometimes desperately – to find ways of differentiating themselves from other brands offering almost the same thing at more or less the same price. Whether or not this is a sensible business strategy is a fundamental question (and we shall return to it in Chapters 3 and 5).

Nevertheless, an identifying difference is central to the brand. This difference may be built up over a long time, and can give products meaning and direction (Kapferer, 1992). For example, Citroën cars – going back to the pre-war Traction Avant models and through later classics such as the 2CV and DS – are definitely different in their engineering design and sometimes different in their styling. The heritage of Citroën is clear, and it may be argued that in a market in which most cars are becoming more and more alike, it is this heritage alone that will guarantee the company a future – functionality and quality being taken for granted in cars now.

As Kapferer points out, the brand can give meaning and direction even when, as is common, the products are actually identical. For example, anti-lock braking systems (ABS) and many other components are the same across cars, but the brands BMW and Volvo give them completely different significance. For BMW, ABS brakes mean enhanced performance; for Volvo it means even greater safety.

WHAT SHOULD BRAND OWNERS DO?

The fundamentals of brand building have suggested themselves during our discussion. The first and by far the most important fundamental is *to provide superior consumer value*. This could indeed be seen as the basic rationale for the firm's existence. As Peter Drucker pointed out many years ago, the only purpose of a business is to create a customer – and you do that by providing better value than anyone else.

What exactly constitutes superior value then becomes the 64-million-dollar question. The firm must develop *deep understanding of the customer*. Although many companies pay lip service to the idea, their practice often does not back it up. To achieve real empathy with the target market takes more than market research. It means people throughout the company putting themselves in customers' shoes, understanding their problems, seeing the world the way they do, using the product in the way they do. It means analysis and objectivity, but also creativity – sometimes making a leap to predict what consumers will want when it is offered to them.

It also means a total commitment to *quality*. The quality may not be what everyone understands by the term superficially: McDonald's provides superb quality in their service, even though many middle-class critics are condescending towards the food. Quality here must always mean quality as perceived by the consumer – and that is not necessarily what is produced by a 'total quality management' movement in the factory.

In providing this quality, the firm must find some way of *differentiation*. Brand managers and their colleagues probably spend more time on searching for the *point of difference* than in many other aspects of branding. In today's crowded markets, it is increasingly important that the brand offers something that consumers can identify that makes it different. The more mature the market, and the more functionally similar the products on offer, the more vital it is that your brand can give the consumer a handle, a reason for buying. It involves defining what the brand's *core values* are – what it stands for, whom it is for (see Chapter 4). Then, because we expect the brand to last many years, we must look not only for *consistency*, but also for *evolution*. Brands that chop and change merely confuse and alienate consumers. Volvo has a strong positioning because over many years it has been committed to safety above all. On the other hand, no brand can stay still; times change, markets change, and even the strongest brand must change with them. A major challenge is how to update and improve a brand without losing the faithful customers who have loved it for years.

Finally, the firm must *support* its brands. The support may be in the form of heavy above-the-line advertising (as in traditional fmcg markets), in thorough staff training (eg British Airways) or in spending on research and development (eg Sony). No brand can survive for long without the commitment and support of the whole company from the top down.

> The CEO of any company that is heavily invested in brands who does not believe that responsibility for the drama of brand leadership needs to be near the top of his or her personal agenda will have abrogated his or her company's right to brand early in the new millennium. (Macrae, 1996)

To that battle cry, I would add that many firms who are not currently heavily invested in brands will need to be in future, since their global competitors certainly will be.

2

The Value of Brands

In the first chapter, it was taken for granted that strong brands were worth having. In this section we will examine the evidence for this, since building and maintaining a brand necessarily involve large expenditures. Are we sure that it is worth it, assuming of course that the effort is successful? The evidence falls into a number of categories: that from the longevity of some brands, from various sorts of market data and from takeovers. We will then look at some of the issues arising from the attempt to place monetary value on brands, and at the whole concept of brand equity.

LONG-LIVED BRANDS

We noted in Chapter 1 that some brands have very long lives. Some, such as Coca-Cola or Gillette, date from the 19th century. In both the United States and the UK, many brands have led their category for 60 years or more (see Table 2.1).

The longevity of these brands – and the profits they have earned over their lifetimes – are not accidental. They are all leaders because: they have offered consistent high quality, equal to or better than any competitor; they have been supported by heavy investment in manufacturing and marketing (advertising and distribution); and they have adapted to changes in consumer tastes, either through research and development and/or through

Table 2.1 *Leading brands in the United States and the UK since 1933*

US Brands		UK Brands	
Brand	*Market*	*Brand*	*Market*
Eastman Kodak	cameras/film	Hovis	bread
Del Monte	canned fruit	Kellogg's	cornflakes
Wrigley	chewing gum	Gillette	razors
Nabisco	biscuits	Schweppes	mixers
Gillette	razors	Colgate	toothpaste
Campbell's	soups	Kodak	film
Ivory	soap	Hoover	vacuum cleaners
Coca-Cola	soft drinks	Brooke Bond	tea
Goodyear	tyres		

Source: Interbrand

changes in product formulation, packaging or positioning. It is certain that the managers of the producing firms have seen the maintenance of their brand's leading position as a major strategic objective, and they have kept their eye on the ball.

Evidence from the Profit Impact of Market Strategy (PIMS) study – the largest database of business results in the world – shows that market leadership is highly related to *perceived quality*, and the long-lived brands listed above are testimony to that.

MARKET LEADERSHIP AND PROFITABILITY

Several pieces of evidence as to the profitability of strong brands were gathered together by Peter Doyle (1989):

■ Brands with a market share of 40 per cent generate three times the return on investment of those with a share of only 10 per cent.
■ For UK grocery brands, the number one brand generates over six times the return on sales of the number two brand, while the number three and four brands are unprofitable.
■ For US consumer goods, the number one brand earned a 20 per cent return, the number two earned around 5 per cent and the rest lost money.

▓ Small brands can be profitable: a strong brand in a niche market earns a higher return than a strong brand in a big market. In large markets, competitive threats and retailer pressure can hold back profits even for the top brand.

▓ Premium brands earn 20 per cent more than discount brands.

▓ It can cost six times as much to win new customers as to retain current ones.

▓ Best feasible strategy to achieve profitability and growth is to focus on brand differentiation rather than on cost and price. Although the best strategy in theory is both low cost and high differentiation, it is worth paying some cost penalty to achieve strong differentiation.

These are enormously powerful lessons. They should be engraved in large letters and framed above the desks of marketing directors and, perhaps more important, finance directors in every company which has – or thinks it ought to have – brands. The results relate only to fmcg brands, but the evidence from the PIMS study shows that, across a wide range of industries, the biggest factor relating to high profitability is market share.

If it is argued that the findings are only about market leaders, and strong brands, then that underlines the message of this book: *firms should aim for strong brands that dominate their market segment*.

Companies that want to be leaders must strive to dominate the large, central segments that account for most volume; but niche brands can also be profitable, as long as they are strong in their chosen target area.

Another study compared, over a 20-year period, companies relying mainly on heavily branded goods with those that derive their value independently from brands: the branded firms consistently outperformed the others on the FTSE 350 stock exchange index (Ward and Perrier, 1998).

In an especially intriguing comparison, Almquist, Turvill and Roberts (1998) showed what happened when General Motors (GM) and Toyota both marketed a car produced by them both in a joint venture. The cars were functionally identical, but branded as 'Geo Prizm' and 'Toyota' respectively. Between 1990 and 1994, Toyota sold 200,000 Corollas at US $11,000 each, while GM could sell no more than 80,000 – and at a lower price of US $10,700. Toyota made over US $100 million more than GM, and its dealers made a further US $128 million. The difference can be attributed only to the greater power of the Toyota brand over GM's. That may well be related to perceptions of greater product quality, based on experience, reports and word of mouth; but however it arose, it clearly demonstrates the financial value of a superior brand.

TAKEOVERS

The first time brands became headline news in the UK was when Nestlé made a takeover bid for Rowntree, the well-known confectionery manufacturer. The amount Nestlé was willing to pay pushed the Rowntree share price from 475p to 1075p. The total paid meant that assets as valued in the company's accounts amounted to only 17 per cent of the price – so it was clear that Nestlé was paying a huge premium for the value of Rowntree's brands. Other takeovers in Europe and the United States gave a similar message.

Carlo de Benedetti bought Buitoni, a poorly-performing Italian food manufacturer, for less than £100 million in 1985. Three years later, he sold Buitoni on to Nestlé for £800 million. In the meantime, he had established the potential for Buitoni to launch a range of European brands. Multiples of earnings paid for brand-rich acquisitions ranged from 25 to 41 – at a period when price/earnings ('p/e') ratios were much lower than they are today. Such prices could not possibly be justified by the company's recent records.

What were these sophisticated buyers paying such enormous sums *for*? There are three underlying reasons:

▓ The buyers were paying, not for the current performance of the brands, but for their *future potential*; Nestlé has made KitKat into a truly European brand, with greatly improved sales and still further potential for future expansion.
▓ There are very few possible takeover targets in these crowded but lucrative markets; the acquirers were paying a premium *to prevent competitors from getting the brands*.
▓ It is easier to buy successful brands than to build them from scratch.

In some cases, it seems likely that a considerable degree of over-bidding was present, but only time will tell whether the assets acquired were a bargain or an expensive white elephant.

BRANDS AND THE BALANCE SHEET

Results such as those quoted above, and takeovers such as those described suggested to many that, if brands really are so valuable, they should be shown on the balance sheet. This idea was particularly attractive to some British companies who perhaps felt vulnerable to takeover attempts themselves and who wanted to strengthen their balance sheets. Others – who had spent the vast sums on acquisitions – wanted to make the best of presenting the results. The outcome has been a debate across Europe and the United States on how brands should be accounted for. An international solution is needed, since many if not most of the companies contemplating the issue are multinationals. It seems likely that an agreed model will emerge.

We need not enter into the technical details of the accounting arguments, but we will touch on a few of the main points. For brands acquired in a takeover, the difference between the price paid for the acquired company and the assets shown in its balance sheet is known as *goodwill*, and this is assumed to include the value of the brands. It is the treatment of this amount that gives rise to the controversy: accounting rules in different countries allow different interpretations.

In some countries, the rules stipulate that the goodwill should be shown as an asset and written off against profits over a period ranging from 4 to 40 years. This will have an immediate effect on apparent profitability. In the UK, the goodwill has often been written off against reserves – which avoids continuing charges against the profit and loss account but takes a one-time hit. Assets are not increased, and indeed shareholders may appear to be worse off after the takeover than before.

One way to get round this is to show the acquired brands on the balance sheet by classifying part of the goodwill as an asset. This is still controversial, for the reasons discussed below on how to value brands.

In Britain, Rank Hovis McDougall were the first to try to extend this idea from brands for which a price had been paid to those which they already owned, that is, those they had developed themselves. The logic is appealing: if brands have real value – and obviously they do since companies are willing to pay very large sums for them – then they have that value all the time, not just when a firm is taken over. Moreover, the addition of new assets in the form of brands will strengthen the balance sheet, which has other attractive results – including making the firm look much more expensive to a predator. However, the concept gives rise to many problems, not least the valuation method.

The Accounting Standards Board in the UK published a new standard in 1997, FRS 10, which allowed acquired brands to be capitalized on a fair value basis – as long as sufficient goodwill is available. Such brand valuations must be checked annually for impairment. The Board also stated that home-grown brands *cannot* be capitalized, since in their view, 'It is not possible to determine a market value for unique intangible assets such as brands...' (paragraph 12).

Whether or not brands will be shown on the balance sheet, it seems entirely reasonable to want to know what they are worth. Only then can sensible judgments be made as to how much it is worth investing in them and how well the investment is being managed. Brand valuation is playing an increasing role in attempts to measure the effectiveness of marketing expenditure; there are, however, many problems.

METHODS OF VALUING BRANDS

The US magazine *Financial World* has a paid circulation of over 500,000 readers. On 2 August 1994 it reported results of a brand valuation survey carried out by *Financial World* staff.

> Here's a shock: the IBM brand name is now worthless. That's just one thing we discovered in valuing 290 of the world's most popular brands. Of the 290 brands we surveyed, 14 had negative or zero value... In such cases, a competing generic product could have generated high profits on the same level of sales.
>
> (Macrae, 1996, p 213)

This finding, nonsensical as it may appear, shows the problems in valuing brands. The method used in the *Financial World* survey is not clear, but it seems to hinge on analysts' views about the strategic competence of firms' managements. IBM has certainly had its problems, but to say that its brand name is now worth nothing seems to fly in the face of common sense. As we now know, IBM has made a successful recovery from its crisis, and is once again a powerful and profitable brand.

How then can we go about valuing brands? The main approach is the accounting/economic method.

Accounting/economic method

The value of an asset is that it can provide a stream of future earnings. Because accounting rules stress conservatism and factual accuracy, the traditional way of valuing assets has been the historic cost: you know exactly what you paid for an asset, and there can be no doubts about it. Assets that lose their value over time are depreciated, that is, their cost is amortized over what is thought to be their useful life. It is this approach that has been used in takeovers to value brands, but with the problems of overbidding mentioned above. The stock market is supposed to be an efficient processor of information, so in theory the value of brands should be built into every company's share price already. If a predator disagrees with the stock market's valuation and is prepared to pay a premium, that introduces an element of subjectivity. Different predators will have different views on the price worth paying, that is, on the value of brands. Accountants are, not surprisingly, unhappy with this.

An alternative approach is to estimate not the actual historic cost of an asset, but its replacement cost; this became popular during periods of high inflation when historic costs were thought to be misleading. It is readily apparent that applying this method to brands also introduces a large subjective element. We know so little about market behaviour – except that it is dynamic – that estimating the cost of building a new brand from scratch would produce very wide margins of error indeed.

A final problem is that known as *separability*, which refers to the difficulty of knowing exactly what belongs to the brand and what belongs to other parts of the company. If for example the brand name alone is sold – as it often is – this gives the buyer the right to use the name and any trademarks, patents etc. It does not transfer physical assets such as factories, or other factors such as manufacturing know-how and distribution strength. How much of the brand's success and future potential belong to the brand as such, and how much to these other factors? It is of course such calculations that lead different companies to put different values on other firms' brands. It may well be that a brand is worth much more to Nestlé than to a small local producer because Nestlé's skills and market power will offer the brand very much better chances on a European or world scale. However, it is clear that such issues will make estimates of value wide-ranging, and not conservative or factual.

Finally, it could be argued that if the value of a brand is its stream of potential future earnings, then the way to estimate its value is to calculate those earnings directly – suitably deflated to a net present value. By now it should be clear that, however sophisticated the models used to do this, some subjectivity and uncertainty will necessarily be present. The estimates produced may be mathematically impressive, but the range of uncertainty built into them is just as wide. There is also the problem of separating the future profits that would be earned by the investment up to now and those earned by future marketing expenditure. If the valuation is used from year to year to measure the effectiveness of marketing effort, then assumptions may change – and that will critically alter brand valuation. These and other difficulties (see Ambler and Barwise, 1998) are considerable, but this is not to argue that no such models should be developed, rather that they will not solve the accounting problem.

Other methods

Any attempt to model future sales and market share will recognize that multiple factors are involved. Many approaches therefore explicitly list the factors assumed to cause sales and market share, and quantify them. The technique has been widely used, especially in the UK and increasingly in the United States. (Some models will be described briefly in the next section on brand equity.) Interbrand used such an approach for many years, and it was widely applied; the fact that it has now been abandoned suggests that the problems of subjectivity inherent in the model made it unreliable.

Other methods include the use of consumer attitudes, the premium price that a brand can charge, estimated royalty income and momentum accounting. Brand valuation is such a growing industry that all the big five accountants – and other types of consultant – have their own models (Ambler and Barwise, 1998).

BRAND EQUITY

In recent years, the debate about the value of brands has been crystallized in the phrase 'brand equity' – except that crystallized is probably the wrong word, since the concept is anything but sharp and crystal clear. The phrase is used in varying ways, and seldom precisely.

Let us start then with one attempt to be clear. Aaker defines brand equity as: 'a set of assets and liabilities linked to a brand, its name and symbol, that add value or subtract from the value provided by a product or service to a firm and/or to that firm's customers' (Aaker, 1991, p 15). He goes on to say that these assets and liabilities can be grouped under five categories:

1. brand loyalty;
2. name awareness;
3. perceived quality;
4. brand associations in addition to perceived quality; and
5. other proprietary brand assets – patents, trademarks, channel relationships, etc. His model is shown in Figure 2.1.

The difficulty that many people – including this author – have with Aaker's model is the same as we have with many similar marketing models. No one would disagree that the factors listed – brand loyalty and so on – are in themselves good things. We would rather have them than be without them. The difficulty is that there is absolutely no evidence that they are related systematically to brand equity – whatever that is.

We can, using market research, measure the factors listed and obtain ratings of how consumers view a brand. What we do not know is what to do with them next. Are the factors weighted

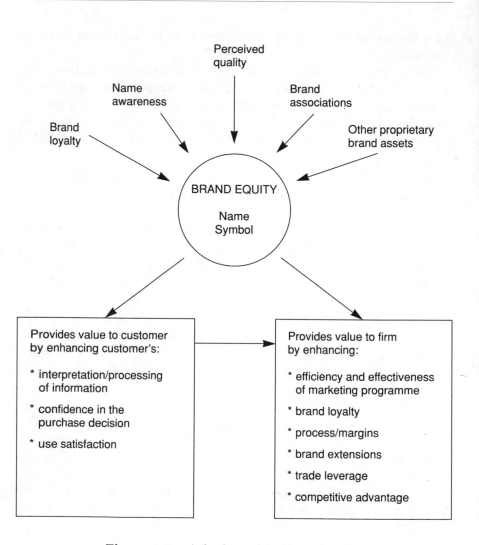

Figure 2.1 *Aaker's model of brand equity*

differently and, if so, how? Do the weights vary between different product fields, and even different brands? How exactly do the ratings translate into 'confidence in the purchase decision' or 'use satisfaction'?

Ironically, Aaker provides an example of the difficulties in obtaining valid data later in his book. Users of insurance services in California were asked to give satisfaction ratings using return cards. By such measures, the firms in the insurance industry – with over 95 per cent approval – looked good just prior to the passing of Proposition 103, which mandated a 20 per cent reduction in insurance rates in California.

To be fair, Aaker points out the validity problem, but having stated the problem does not go on to solve it (Aaker, 1991, p 45).

Ambler and Barwise (1998) define brand equity as 'the marketing asset that exists in customers' minds and is of continuing value to the brand owner because it influences future purchases by the buyer and the buyer's social network through word of mouth'. In a similar vein, Srivastava and Shocker (1991) define it as 'a set of associations and behaviours on the part of a brand's customers, channel members and parent corporation that permits the brand to earn greater volume or greater margins than it could without the brand name and that gives a strong, sustainable and differential advantage.' While this rightly draws attention to the key aspects of consumers, future purchasing and profits, it could equally stand as a definition of a brand, and it does not take us much further in attempting to measure brand equity.

The other attempts to measure brand equity take a generally similar approach to Aaker's; they are summarized in Table 2.2.

It can be seen that some use relatively 'hard' measures such as market share and relative price, while others use 'softer' units such as liking or perceived quality. The test for all of them will be to show over time that they can produce valuable data that managers can use. All are subject to the criticism levelled above at Aaker's model. We can sum up this complicated and messy area as follows:

■ Brands clearly have a value, since some companies are prepared to pay large sums for the privilege of acquiring them.
■ All the methods of trying to estimate the value of an individual brand are fraught with difficulties.
■ The concept of brand equity is used in different ways to try to capture the idea that a brand has a value.
■ However, no valid, reliable way of measuring brand equity has yet emerged; that is, no one method is guaranteed to produce a valid result for a particular case.

This does not imply that the methods proposed are without merit, nor that managers should not try to measure the value of their brands. As suggested above, it seems eminently sensible to do just that. Rather than argue vaguely about the long-term value of a

Table 2.2 *Measures of brand equity*

Name	Supplier	Description
Image Power	Landor Associates	Familiarity, esteem
Equitrend	Total Research Corp.	Quality perceptions (11-point scale)
The Conversion Model	Market Facts	Willingness to continue buying
Equity Monitor	Yankelovich	Factors that create equity – attitude, behaviour, economic
Unnamed	DDB Needham	Brand awareness × liking × perceived quality
Brand Equity Index	Longman Moran	Market share × relative price × durability
Consumer Brand Equity	Leo Burnett	Sales, price, distribution
Brand Asset (TM)	Young and Rubicam	Differentiation × relevance = vitality Esteem × familiarity = magnitude/stature All = brand asset

Source: Ambler, 1995

strong brand or the need to treat brand advertising as an investment, surely it would be better to have at least some idea of what value we have built up already; then we can begin to measure the effect of our actions on maintaining or increasing that value.

This is not to underestimate the problems of such measurement; these have already been noted above. However, unless we start somewhere, we will never be any the wiser. Systematic collection and analysis of data over many years may bring enlightenment. Some of the uncertainties will remain, as that is the nature of marketing. However, an explicit model of exactly how we believe we are adding value will help us think, argue marketing's case with the accountants, and perhaps even strengthen our reputation in the City (ie the financial district of London). At the very least, it will get people from different functions in the firm talking about the same thing and developing a common language. If, as this book argues, strong brands are central to companies' survival and growth, then that alone would be worth the candle.

3

Challenges to Brands

The first two chapters concentrated on the power and attractiveness of brands. They do not, of course, have the world all their own way. Indeed, in recent years, many commentators have suggested that the heyday of the brand is over; some have even predicted 'the death of brands'. The view taken here is that this is a gross overreaction, but there is no doubt that brands are facing serious challenges that – if not recognized and met with positive action – will probably lead to the death of *some* brands that today take their continuing existence for granted. In this chapter, we will examine those challenges.

Many of the threats we need to face are interrelated. They are, in summary:

- mature markets;
- brand proliferation;
- consumer revolt;
- management failures;
- fragmentation of media; and
- retailer power.

MATURE MARKETS

Many if not most consumer markets are in their mature stage, showing only marginal growth that reflects population increase or the economic cycle. There are some exceptions, but as John Philip Jones points out:

> This lack of market vitality appears irreversible since it represents a seemingly permanent ceiling on consumers' purchase levels in all except a few areas – mainly financial and other services and high tech, not the traditional categories of packaged goods and consumer durables.
>
> (Jones, 1990)

Even in fields such as consumer electronics that have for many years shown exceptional buoyancy, the drying up of innovative new products has left giants such as Sony and Matsushita struggling. Nor should firms in business-to-business and industrial markets feel too complacent, since much of their demand is necessarily derived – directly or indirectly – from consumer markets.

Since a company cannot simply change its whole area of operations overnight, it must look hard and carefully at its prospects. As subsequent comments will make clear, finding growth in mature markets is difficult at any time, but the problems are complicated by the other factors discussed.

BRAND PROLIFERATION

The classic response of marketing departments to the challenge of low growth has been to extend the brand with new varieties, or to develop new brands. For a time this seemed to be an effective strategy, but in the 1990s it may have become self-defeating.

> I began thinking about this in earnest a couple of years ago while shopping in a nearby supermarket. I came upon a couple – well-dressed, alert-looking, possibly in their late forties. They appeared to me to be everything that a marketer would want in potential customers, and more.
>
> This couple was doing their best to buy a bottle of Bayer aspirin. There was no doubt that their brand choice had long since been made; they were looking only at the array of Bayer brand variants. But they were clearly puzzled about which Bayer brand variant to buy. There were eight on the shelf, each with different modifying descriptors and each with apparently different characteristics. One of the Bayer variants was offered by the retailer at a 'special' price, yet it

was still priced somewhat higher than the other variants. In addition, five of the Bayer variants had a package flag explaining that either the product or the package label itself was 'new'.

(Weilbacher, 1993)

The story ends with the couple – puzzled by the variety of similar and in fact therapeutically identical products – buying a rival brand. The moral is obvious, but how many brand and marketing managers will be squirming as they read this? The pressures on managers (discussed below) and the dynamics of the marketing system have made such developments apparently inevitable.

Bill Weilbacher (1993) goes on to point out that in an average US supermarket you could find, to take just two examples from many, 12 varieties of Campbell's chicken noodle soup and no less than 10 brands of blue cheese salad dressing alone.

The situation in the United States has been extreme in that the huge and growing size of typical supermarkets has produced extra shelf space that has allowed – even encouraged – such proliferation. In Japan, where retailers are co-operative or heavily influenced by manufacturers, 1,000 new soft drinks brands were launched in one year, with 99 per cent failing (de Chernatony and McDonald, 1992). In Europe – and particularly in the UK, where land is scarce and expensive – this has not been true; indeed to some extent the opposite has been the case (see below).

The principle remains applicable, however. Because genuine innovations are so hard to find in mature markets, manufacturers rely on introductions of 'new' products that are all too often minor variations on existing ones. This is not to belittle real improvements; firms dedicated to quality products and customer service will always be striving to make their offering that little bit better. The doubts remain over the many instances in which it appears that the manufacturer is making a distinction without a difference, merely to try to differentiate the brand from competitors. According to one study, consumers are 'extremely irritated' by the plethora of products that can make buying a toothbrush or a shampoo into an unnecessary drama (*Financial Times*, 10 December 1999). One in three consumers interviewed said that there was too much choice and 90 per cent said that manufacturers routinely over-claimed about all new products. The criticisms extend beyond fmcg to telecoms and high-technology companies.

The US magazine *Business Week* publishes an annual survey of the 'Best New Products'. From the 38 noted for the years 1989, 1990 and 1991, there were 22 brand refinements, 13 market segmenters or brand extensions and 3 genuine product innovations (ie a Black and Decker steam wallpaper stripper, a new prescription drug and a Tandy computer that accepts handwritten inputs) (Weilbacher, 1993, p 40). These, it should be stressed, were the *best* new products over three years, so you can imagine what the rest – many thousands of them – were like.

The marketing people responsible for all this activity were of course only putting into practice what has been assumed to be 'correct' marketing of brands. You differentiate your brand, segment the market and introduce extensions as 'flankers' to block competitors or to fill out your line. The problem is that the markets have become too crowded; there aren't any more real niches to discover, and competitors are all too ready to jump on any bandwagon that seems to be rolling in more or less the right direction. Brand proliferation is a self-inflicted wound.

The whole area of brand extensions is extremely important and firms cannot simply forswear it. (We will return to this subject in more detail in Chapter 5.)

CONSUMER REVOLT

The same commentators who were proclaiming the death of the brand were blaming it on a revulsion by consumers against the excesses of the 1980s. People in the caring 1990s, it is said, are sceptical of over-claiming by brands, fed up with paying a premium for non-existent differences and looking for real value for money.

The second of April 1993 became known as 'Marlboro Friday' because on that day Philip Morris announced a 20 per cent price cut on its famous cigarette brand. Reaction to such drastic action by what had been seen as one of the world's premier brands led to billions of US dollars being wiped off the stock market value not only of Philip Morris but also of many other fmcg companies.

What on earth was going on? Philip Morris was reacting to a steady erosion of Marlboro's market share by cut-price generic cigarettes; in the previous nine months the generics' growth had sped up and they had reached 36 per cent of the market. Philip

Morris accepted lower profits in the short run to regain its market share – which at the time of writing it seemed likely to accomplish. There are several interpretations of these events.

What the stock market appeared to think was that the days of brands able to charge a premium were well and truly over. Consumers had changed dramatically and permanently, and brand owners would never again be able to earn their previous level of profit.

An alternative view was that Philip Morris had been greedy: it had consistently raised prices by more than inflation, thereby leaving itself open to attack by the discount products (see for example Randall, 1994, p 14). Consumers were willing to pay a premium for the additional benefits of the brand, even though these were entirely psychological benefits; but there was a limit, and the premium had simply become too high.

On the other hand, it is possible to argue that even if this were true, Philip Morris had made millions of US dollars in extra profits during the years it had been charging the premium, so it was much better off than if it had been more sensitive to consumer feelings. This hypothesis could be tested by financial modelling, but in any case expresses a branding philosophy that can perhaps be summed up as, 'It's all right to screw your consumers as long as they will put up with it.' That philosophy is firmly rejected by this book.

Finally, it has been suggested that Philip Morris was playing a finely judged, deep, competitive game. Its main competitor, R J Reynolds, was financially insecure; Philip Morris lulled it into a false sense of security, then introduced the drastic price cut knowing that it would hurt Reynolds far more than themselves (Macrae, 1996, p 125). If you believe in the conspiracy theory of history, you may believe this.

How much other reliable evidence is there that consumers are turning away from brands? There is some data showing that in certain fields major brands are tending to lose market share and that the total number of brands bought has increased. Other figures show a decline in consumers' perceptions of brand differences:

The advertising agency BBDO asked consumers throughout the world in thirteen categories of goods whether they felt the products they had to choose from were more or less the same. The per cent who indicated brand parity ranged from 52 per cent for cigarettes to 76 per cent for credit cards. It was noticeably higher for such products as paper towels and dry soup, which emphasise performance benefits, than for products like cigarettes, coffee and beer, for which imagery has been the norm.

(Aaker, 1991, p 10)

To some extent this reaction merely reflects the brand proliferation mentioned above. If manufacturers continue to fill the shelves with brands that are essentially the same as all the others, then it is hardly surprising that consumers notice.

Whether there is genuinely a serious, permanent switch away from branded products to unbranded ones is more questionable. The period in which this was claimed to be happening was one of recession in most countries, and it is quite normal during recessionary times for consumers to draw in their horns. Greatly increased caution has marked many areas of consumer spending in recent years, reflecting the much greater level of uncertainty people feel about their future job security. In such conditions, they may decide not to spend discretionary income or, if they do, to wait for the sales. Luxury brands are often immune – since the rich are relatively less affected by economic downturns – but premium brands may find their consumers deserting them for so-called 'value brands'. The question is, will they return when economic conditions improve? In some fields, the late 1990s suggested that they will not. In clothing, 'value' chains such as Matalan made impressive gains, while the middle market players such as Marks & Spencer and Arcadia suffered. As quality retailing brands (eg Next) continue to prosper, it may be that a U-shaped market is developing – with the top and bottom attracting customers and the middle declining. The pattern is not general, however, and in electronic goods, for example, customers are spending as before. Suppliers and retailers will have to watch their own sector closely to discern the trends there.

It must be true that strong brands always have to offer perceived value for money, and well-managed brands make sure that they do – even if sometimes they have to remind consumers of the fact, as Fairy Liquid has been doing in recent years. In crowded, competitive, mature markets consumers are sophisticated and knowledgeable, but a brand that offers them reassurance and familiarity – *provided that it is seen to give acceptable value for money* – can continue to attract. (Further discussion on how consumers use brands is given in Chapter 4.)

MANAGEMENT FAILURES

The main areas in which managements themselves represent a threat to their brands are: short-termism, greed, neglect, and weak marketing. These are often interrelated, but let us look at them separately.

Short-termism

The argument that the Anglo-Saxon business world – that is, the United States and the UK – is forced by the stock market to take a much shorter-term view of company strategy than their competitors in, say, Germany and Japan is too well known to need rehearsing here. Some critics deny it, but most evidence suggests that managers feel intense pressure to produce the quarterly numbers. In highly volatile and turbulent times – such as many industries have experienced recently – short-term survival could be seen as the only sensible approach.

A more insidious influence has been top management compensation plans. Widespread publicity has shown that in many companies top managers have received significantly increased rewards, almost regardless of how well their companies are actually doing. These payments have usually resulted from plans that reward the achievement of specific, normally financial, objectives such as share price or earnings per share. It is perhaps not surprising that human nature has dictated that managers concentrate on producing results that give them personally the rewards promised – however short-term the resulting decisions.

Most managers would accept that they need to think beyond this quarter and this year if they are to be able to offer continuing, sustainable consumer value better than their competitors. The pressure on short-term numbers, however, means that longer-term strategy has to be sacrificed. One example is in the area of advertising and promotion; where short-term corporate decisions affect marketing policy, it seems that long-term marketing thinking has suffered. This point will be developed under the section on weak marketing below.

Greed

Consider again the Philip Morris case described in the section on consumer revolt above. On one interpretation – and the one favoured here – it was a classic example of the greed that managements can display. The point of a strong brand is to be able to charge a premium and to make good profits; on that we must agree. But the objective must always be to provide superior consumer value, and that cannot be done by milking the brand. Obviously the short-term pressures already described are also at work here, but they must be resisted – and it is up to the marketing people to do so.

Neglect

Top managements have been under enormous pressures over the last few years. They have had to face dramatic technological change, economic upheaval, increasing competition (often international, sometimes brutal), potential takeover threats, new regulations from governments and supra-governmental bodies, consumer protests and now e-commerce – they could probably add more to their list of pressures. They have reacted by introducing downsizing, total quality management, just-in-time delivery, business process re-engineering and all the other management panaceas touted by consultants. In the process, they have neglected brands.

> Is it asking too much of them to insist that they should still be concentrating on brand values, how to build them, how to maintain them? No, it is not. They are not paid the comparatively large sums that they receive because the job is easy. It is their duty to safeguard the future of the company as well as its present, and that future must depend crucially on strong brands. They will not be thanked for delivering results which please the stock market this year if in the process they destroy the company potential for growth over the next ten – or fifty – years.
>
> (Randall, 1994, p 15)

Weak marketing

' "There is a systemic failure in marketing culture and companies' organizations," says market research consultant David Cowan'

(Mitchell, 1995). During the early 1990s this sort of quotation became common. Reports from management consultants Coopers & Lybrand and McKinsey reported a widespread dissatisfaction on the part of the board members with the performance of marketing departments in large companies. After years of enjoying increasing status, marketing was now under attack.

What went wrong? Marketing people used to be known in Procter and Gamble as 'the housewife's representatives in the company', but it seems that they were failing in that role in many firms. Let us return to the issue of spending on advertising and promotion mentioned earlier.

> Advertising can help to build brands by communicating value and adding personality; nothing else can do the job as well. *Yet brand advertising by manufacturers has been declining in real terms by more than 60 per cent over a period when advertising by retailers increased by 40 per cent.* It has also declined comparatively: while promotion to advertising ratios were about 40/60 in the USA ten years ago, they are now 60/40 and still changing.
>
> (Randall, 1994, p 16)

'In fact the proportion of total marketing expenditures devoted to trade and consumer promotion probably exceeds 70 per cent and may have reached 75 per cent' (Weilbacher, 1993, p 56). The importance of advertising need not be taken for granted. The PIMS database referred to in Chapter 2 has been re-analysed to show the relationship between advertising, market share and profitability. Table 3.1 shows clearly that businesses with high market share tend to spend more on advertising and to have significantly higher return on investment.

The argument can be summarized in a few points:

▨ *advertising* is essential to building consumer perceptions of brand values in most markets;

▨ *but* advertising works in the long term (one to three years) and has relatively little effect on sales in the short term (a disputed point, to which we will return);

▨ *so* heavy expenditure on brand-building advertising – which the marketing people would argue is an investment – is difficult to justify to the accountants and is the budget most likely to be cut in a cash flow crisis;

Table 3.1 *Advertising analysis using PIMS data*

Advertising to Sales Ratio Versus Direct Competitors	Average Share of Market %	Average Return on Investment %
Much less	14	17
Less	20	22
Equal	25	22
More	26	25
Much more	32	32

Source: Re-analysis of PIMS data by WPP, Biel. (Quoted in de Chernatony and McDonald, 1992, p 265)

■ *whereas* below-the-line promotion does have a short-term effect on sales – even though the effect is temporary and may in the end be damaging;
■ *and* retailers are very fond of promotion, as they normally pocket large amounts of it, so they put pressure on manufacturers to spend more below the line – particularly in trade promotion.

So the marketing people have not been strong enough to withstand pressures from two fronts: internally, from accountants and top managers, and externally, from strong retailers. Internal politics seem to have produced common organizational problems in many companies. According to Chris Macrae, these are:

■ A non-entrepreneurial bias.
■ A tendency towards proliferation of brands.
■ The spawning of complex political power battles as managers battle over resources for each brand.
■ The value-destroying syndrome. By apparently delegating brand decisions to junior and rotating brand managers, the system starts to lack continuity of know-how and soon becomes the antithesis of a process which engages genuinely innovative teamwork. (1996, p 253)

The addition, for fmcg companies, of vastly increased retailer power (see below and Chapter 7), has only made it easier simply to abdicate responsibility and rely on promotion and other short-term palliatives to show the sort of results which the bosses want. The health of the brand is bound to suffer.

MEDIA COST AND FRAGMENTATION

If heavy advertising support is essential in the traditional model of the strong consumer brand, the technological and social developments of recent years have looked threatening. The cost of television time has risen much faster than inflation in most countries where it is available at all. Developments such as cable and satellite systems now offer enormous choice, thereby fragmenting audiences. This is further exacerbated by 'time-shifting' through video-recorders, which also allow viewers to 'zap' unwanted commercial breaks.

Future developments offer potentially even more choice, with literally hundreds of channels, and video-on-demand or something very like it. New media have proliferated: 'I am constantly bombarded with offers to advertise here, support this, sponsor that' (Chris Hobbs of 3M, quoted in Macrae, 1996, p 106). Computer databases and new methods of analysis offer the potential for highly targeted campaigns directed at individuals – that is, 'one-to-one marketing'.

Partly as a consequence of – and partly as the enabling cause of – this fragmentation, audiences are becoming more segmented. The result, argue some people, is that the old style of mass advertising campaign is no longer possible or desirable. A calmer view is that the challenge of producing an *integrated* communications campaign is now very much more difficult. It may of course also be liberating, allowing new ways of talking to consumers and building the relationship.

RETAILER POWER

In many consumer goods fields in most countries, there has been a huge growth in concentration in retailing. The result is a complete switch in the balance of power between manufacturers and retailers, with the latter now holding the whip hand. The effect on promotional spending has been noted. That is a symptom of a more worrying trend, that of the marketing department spending more of its time and effort trying to please retailers, and less on its one absolutely vital task of understanding and pleasing consumers. (The notion of retailer power has already been mentioned more than once, and will be dealt with at more length in Chapter 7.)

To sum up, nowadays there are unprecedented challenges to the old model of branding. Reports of the death of brands are – in this writer's view – nonsensical, but the severity of the threats cannot be underestimated. Any marketing strategy has to face them, and propose realistic ways of overcoming them. What those ways are will be shown in the later chapters of this book.

4

Consumers and Brands

Although we have repeated several times that the focus of brands must always be the people who buy and use them, so far we have not looked more closely at that relationship. In this chapter we will concentrate on what we actually know about how customers and consumers view brands, how they choose them and how they use them. First we shall try to dispel some common myths.

MISTAKEN ASSUMPTIONS

Because we know comparatively little – scientifically speaking – about human behaviour, we have to make assumptions. This is particularly so in marketing, where most decisions are concerned directly or indirectly with how people will react to what we do. There are many assumptions common in marketing that may or may not be true – and there are some for which there is now reasonable evidence that they are in fact *not* true.

Consumers go through a rational decision process when they buy

This is a common, perhaps flattering assumption. You will still find, in many marketing books, models of buying processes such as 'AIDA' (attention, interest, desire, action). Sometimes they are more complicated and dressed up in academic jargon, but they all assume some process, with stages starting at ignorance and moving through awareness, interest, belief, conviction and so on until the ultimate goal – purchase – is reached. The assumption is further that it is marketing actions that propel people along this scale and persuade them to buy. This model has no basis in fact.

To be fair, we should make a distinction between two basic types of product purchasing: high involvement and low involvement. The great majority of consumer purchases are made in low-involvement situations. Although the managers and staff marketing the product or service are deeply involved in it and notice the tiniest characteristic of everything about it, most buyers do not. Choosing between brands of most frequently bought goods is something we do without thinking too deeply about it. Consider your own shopping habits. How often in a supermarket do you go through a complex decision process – weighing up all the information at your disposal, or seeking more information – before evaluating all the available brands and making a choice which maximizes your personal objectives?

Most buying processes for fmcg are routine and trivial. Buyers have a set of brands in mind, with some preferences probably developed over years. As we shall see below, they buy with discernible patterns that reflect this approach. Given the triviality of the decision and the fact that the consequences of buying one brand rather than another are usually vanishingly small, this is in itself a rational decision-making process. To spend more time on each decision would not make sense, and the less time people have available, the less they want to spend on trivial purchase decisions.

This leaves high-involvement situations. Some consumer purchases, and many in the business world, are anything but trivial. The decision process then is much more likely to resemble the rational models, with stages of information seeking, analysis, evaluation and so on. Even here, the actual amount of information seeking may be rather small (see below).

In these markets, it is extremely important to understand the decision process – especially the information-seeking and evaluation stages – so that you know how, when and to whom to try to communicate your own information. Information that buyers already have stored in their minds assumes great weight if they are not going to seek more. Knowledge of – and attitudes towards – your brand may be the determining influence.

Buyers are brand loyal

The assumption underlying marketing thinking seems to be that consumers are divided into two distinct groups: loyal buyers of my brand and loyal buyers of other brands. The marketing task is to keep existing loyal buyers happy and to tempt buyers of rival brands to become loyal buyers of our brand. This is the rationale for most promotional activity: if we can tempt people to buy our brand once by offering them some extra inducement, some of them will become hooked and remain as new loyal buyers.

In general, however, buyers are not brand loyal. Some of you will immediately be thinking, 'But I *always* buy Brand X, and nothing else will do!' Obviously, we must say that in all markets there will be *some* loyal buyers, and the proportion of loyal buyers will vary between product fields.

The data in Figure 4.1 show the percentage of buyers in a range of fields who claim to be loyal to one brand; the level varies from 71 per cent in cigarettes to 23 per cent in rubbish bags.

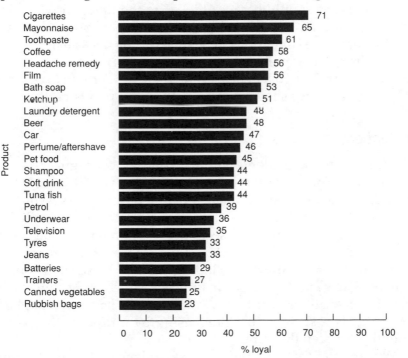

Source: *Wall Street Journal*, 19 October 1989

Figure 4.1 *Users who are loyal to one brand*

However, even these figures are suspect. There can be very few cigarette smokers, for instance, who – having run out late in the evening – will not accept any substitute for their normal brand. Personally, I have used Maclean's toothpaste since I was a child, and really like no others; but at present I am using Signal because we could not find my brand in a French supermarket. Ehrenberg's research, discussed below, shows clearly how these buying patterns are repeated in most markets.

WHAT DO WE KNOW ABOUT HOW CONSUMERS BUY?

Although in this area – as elsewhere in marketing – there is the usual problem that much useful research is not published because it is commercially valuable, there is in practice a body of hard evidence about how consumers actually buy. Most of it is based on fmcg markets, simply because those are the fields in which large amounts of data are collected. Where comparisons are possible, there seem to be similarities in business-to-business markets.

The most comprehensive research programme is that by Ehrenberg and his colleagues. While there is not room to cover it in any real depth, we shall summarize the main points here.

Ehrenberg's findings

Andrew Ehrenberg, along with a variety of colleagues, has been researching consumer buying *behaviour* for over 30 years. He has concentrated on behaviour, that is, actual purchases as recorded by panels of informants over time. These data allow analysis of buying *patterns*, that is, a sequence of purchases over several months or years. The research has covered over 30 product categories in several countries including the UK, Western Europe, the United States and Japan. For reasons explained above, most of the categories were fmcg, but where the methods have been applied to other fields – such as fuel purchasing by airlines – the patterns found have been the same.

We can safely say that this body of evidence is the most comprehensive and soundly based available on how consumers actually buy. The fact that the evidence has been ignored, particularly in the

United States (with honourable exceptions such as Weilbacher, 1993), is disappointing. It seems that marketing people accept 'academic' findings only when they agree with them. There is, of course, nothing academic about Ehrenberg's work; his evidence is fundamental to an understanding of consumers and brands.

The basic finding of Ehrenberg's work is that buying patterns are stable, and common to all product fields examined. The main points can be summarized quickly. They may appear simple, but many marketing people seem to ignore them in practice:

▓ Total sales are explained by: number of buyers × number of buying occasions (or *frequency*) × size of purchase.
▓ The number of consumers buying each brand (its *penetration*) varies, but buying frequency is much more constant. The penetration may vary between 42 per cent and 7 per cent, for example, but the frequency only varies between 2.5 and 3.7 (eg breakfast cereals).
▓ Average frequency is stable over time. This reflects the fact that most markets studied by Ehrenberg were 'stationary' or mature – but so are most markets.
▓ Average brand penetration is also fairly stable. Similarly, this reflects the nature of the markets studied, in which brand shares changed rather little.
▓ Consumers buy a repertoire of brands.

This last point is probably the most important finding, as it contradicts marketers' fondly held beliefs about loyalty. Ehrenberg has shown conclusively that, in all the markets studied, most buyers buy several brands over a period of time. They buy some brands more often than others and some not at all, but they mainly buy a range of acceptable brands. The frequency with which they buy each brand varies from consumer to consumer but, on average, it matches the brand's overall market share. These findings are written up in detail in a large number of publications, and are brought together in the book *Repeat Buying* by A S C Ehrenberg, 1988, to which the reader is referred.

The importance of these findings, particularly that consumers buy a variety of brands, cannot be stressed too strongly. Most buyers have a set of brands that are acceptable to them. They buy some more often than others and their decisions presumably reflect their preferences (or habit). What marketers can influence is the penetration and frequency of a brand; that is, they should try to get as many people as possible to try the brand, and they should try to persuade people to buy this brand more often in preference to others they buy.

This may seem obvious, but these are the *only* things marketing should be trying to do in most markets. Trying to alter basic purchasing frequency or amount bought per purchase occasion is self-defeating. You can persuade people to buy more of the product than usual this period, but they will then buy less next period. This explains the short-term effect of most promotions (discussed further in Chapter 6). What marketers have to work on, then, is obtaining *trial* and increasing *preference*.

In markets which are growing fast or changing in other ways, these rules may not apply – but they are so widespread that it is worth taking them as the standard against which to measure any variation.

Other evidence on buying patterns

Trial and repeat purchase are the two parameters that determine market share. Trial – or penetration – varies more (see above) and is the easier to influence. With new brand introductions, the level of trial peaks within three or four buying cycles, and then drops off to around 80 per cent of the trial level (King, 1990). Therefore it is vital to obtain early and widespread trial; once buying patterns are established, they are very hard to shift.

Heavy buyers account for the majority of purchases. This clearly varies between markets, but in many the so-called 'Pareto' or '80/20' rule is found. This means that 20 per cent of customers account for 80 per cent of sales. The implication here is that you must above all keep these core buyers happy; any attempt to seduce new buyers – or to get existing buyers to buy more often – must not alienate the heavy buyers.

There is a well-known story about the introduction of Maclean's toothpaste to the United States. The then chairman of Beecham's in the UK told his marketing people to launch the brand in the US market, which was clearly a large and attractive one. They of course, being professionals, insisted that they should carry out market research first. They reported back that the results were negative: consumer preference went 80/20 against the brand. The chairman insisted that they repeat the research, and after the same result was reported, overruled their doubts and told them to launch the brand anyway. It was a success. What they found subsequently was that it was true that only 20 per cent of people liked the taste – but they absolutely loved it, and bought it frequently.

Insofar as segments exist in crowded, competitive markets, the distinguishing brand attributes should be established amongst these core buyers – not amongst the total market.

HOW DO CONSUMERS PERCEIVE AND CHOOSE BRANDS?

So far we have concentrated on actual behaviour, and this is all that matters in the end: we are interested in whether people buy our brand or not. To try to influence their behaviour, however, we need to understand how they make their decisions. This is very much more difficult than measuring buying patterns, as we know relatively little about the human mind. We can ask questions about choosing and buying, and people will give answers – but the answers may not mean much. As individuals, we find it difficult to know exactly how we make decisions, and even if we did know at some level, we could not articulate our feelings. What follows attempts to give an objective summary of what we can actually say with any degree of confidence.

Perception of brands

■ *People perceive the brand as a whole.* Psychologists use the word 'gestalt' to describe the way we form concepts *as a whole*, rather than analytically on the basis of lots of separate pieces.

■ *Perception is selective.* All information is filtered through an individual's experience, beliefs and attitudes. Not all the information that is available can be absorbed.

■ *Consumers' perception is the reality.* An airline chairman is quoted as saying, 'Customers think that if there are coffee stains on the flip-down tables, we don't do our engine maintenance right' (Arnold, 1992, p 18).

It is pointless complaining that consumers' beliefs are

irrational or wrong: they are *their* beliefs, and that is all that matters. It is vital to discover what beliefs consumers have, and how they rate different factors in importance. Especially when many products are in fact very similar, buyers can find ways of distinguishing them; but the factors they use may not be those that the supplier expects.

■ *Processes may not be conscious.* Although information may be forgotten, it can still influence decisions. We can produce rationalised explanations of our thinking, but they do not accurately reflect reality.

Without the labels shown, beer drinkers were generally unable to identify the brand they most often drink and expressed no significant difference between brands. In this instance, the schema of attributes to categorize brands was based solely on the physical characteristics of the brands (eg palate, smell and the visual evaluation). When the study was repeated amongst the same drinkers, but this time with the brands labelled, respondents immediately identified their most often drunk brand and commented on significant taste differences between brands! With the labels shown, respondents placed more emphasis on using the brand names to recall brand images as well as their views about how the brands tasted.

(de Chernatony and McDonald, 1992, p 77)

This is one of the most common experiences in branded products: knowledge of the brand identity completely changes consumers' perceptions, even of supposedly objective facts or rational processes.

■ *'The magical number seven, plus or minus two.'* A well-known scientific finding is that humans and other animals can cope with around seven items of information at a time. Most information processing about low-involvement brands probably makes do with rather less than seven items.

■ *The brand has a personality.* Consumers can imagine brands they know well as distinct personalities, with characteristics they can describe. The more complete and balanced the brand identity (see Chapter 1), the richer the consumers' relationship with it, and the better able they are to describe it.

Information-seeking

At the beginning of this chapter we distinguished between the decision processes applied to low- and high-involvement product fields. In the latter, it is generally thought that people do look for information to use in a rational process of choice. For consumer goods – even expensive ones – this search is not as extensive as we might suppose. Consumers are not all readers of *Which?* magazine, and do not necessarily go to great lengths to gather data about a prospective purchase.

> Only five per cent of electrical appliance buyers showed evidence of a very active information search process; a third claimed to seek virtually no pre-purchase information.
>
> Forty-seven per cent of appliance purchasers visited only one store, and only 35 per cent considered another attribute in addition to brand name and price.
>
> A further detailed study of consumers buying cars and major household appliances again showed evidence of limited external search... Forty-four per cent used no more than one information source, 40 per cent experienced a deliberation time of less than two weeks and 49 per cent visited only one retail outlet when making these major brand purchases.
>
> Numerous other instances have been reported of consumers undertaking limited external search for expensive brand purchases in such product fields as financial services, housing, furniture and clothing.
>
> (de Chernatony and McDonald, 1992, p 70)

We can conclude, then, that consumers have large amounts of information available to them, from many different sources – experience, word of mouth, observation, retailers, advertising, press comment and so on. They probably absorb some of it unconsciously, and certainly selectively. They appear to use very little in routine, low-involvement purchases. In grocery stores, for example, 25 per cent make a purchase decision without any time for deliberation and 56 per cent spend less than eight seconds examining and deciding which brand to buy, according to de Chernatony and McDonald (1992). They look for surprisingly little even where there is more at stake, that is, in buying expensive, long-lasting items. In any case, they cannot cope with more than a few items of information at a time. The implications for marketing are that brand messages must be simple and focused.

The position in industrial markets is sometimes different (as we shall see in Chapter 10). Even there, we can assume that routine, low-value purchases follow the consumer pattern.

We will now go on to look at what research methods we can use to find out how buyers think and act in our own market.

MARKETING INFORMATION AND RESEARCH

If we are to focus on customers and consumers – trying to provide what will delight them – and building a relationship between our brand and them, then we need information. Equally, it follows from our earlier insistence that branding involves the whole company that marketing information should not remain the property of the market research department or even the marketing function alone, but should be widely available to all the people who contribute to the delivery of customer satisfaction. Closeness to the customer is a hallmark of successful companies, and each firm needs to work out for itself how to ensure that *everybody* maintains a real understanding of customer needs.

In some firms – Marks & Spencer, for example – all senior managers have to spend some time regularly on the shop floor. At ServiceMaster, managers continue to work at the operational end – actually cleaning customer premises – for a period every year. In some manufacturing companies, groups of shop floor workers visit their customers to see their products in use. This is the most basic form of marketing information, fundamental to understanding customers and therefore central to branding.

Before moving on to more conventional market research, we should note some difficulties with it. All sensible managers know that information – whether about marketing or other aspects of the firm's operations – will not make decisions for them; information is only an aid to better decision-making. With market research for branding, there are more serious problems.

Problems with market research
Absence of valid models
When we discussed what we understand of consumers' motivation and decision processes, it became clear that we know very little about the human mind. Certainly we have no valid models with which to calculate exactly how consumers will react to given marketing actions such as a particular campaign. If consumers'

mental processes are partly unconscious – as we know they are – then we would need techniques to burrow beneath the conscious level to reveal the 'true' thinking taking place. No such techniques exist in a valid, reliable form.

Techniques produce 'answers'

Due to the fact that market researchers are professionals, they will, when asked, carry out research and produce answers for their marketing colleagues. Individuals, when asked questions by researchers, will give answers. The problem is, what do these answers really mean? The following damning description of what actually happens in a typical group discussion was written by a professional researcher with many years' experience. (A group discussion consists of six to eight respondents, hopefully representative of the target market, who are led in a discussion by a trained interviewer.)

> Some sort of brand ... variant is presented to a group of consumers, and they are asked to respond to it. Often enough, the variant ... is some trivial re-slicing of old advertising or brand development baloney.
>
> The respondents, in the social situation created by the group itself, believe that they are expected to take all this seriously. Instead of appearing stupid before their peers and their interrogators, the respondents will respond at will, arguing and challenging each other, randomly articulating whatever seemingly reasonable and socially acceptable thoughts come to mind...
>
> Meanwhile, the marketers listen with rapt attention, grasping at each consumer insight and provocative statement, seeking always a justification for their next marketing action in the words of the beguiled respondents.
>
> (Weilbacher, 1993, p 139)

In other words, the research technique forces answers, but those answers may or may not represent consumer reality – and there is no way of telling.

The other class of research technique that carries a similar danger is that of multivariate analysis, especially when applied to segmentation studies. In order to find segments in a market, researchers will often throw a huge mass of consumer data – on buying habits, attitudes to brands, general attitudes, beliefs, opinions, lifestyle, personality – into a computer program. This will apply complicated statistical techniques and, because it is designed to find segments or clusters, that is what it will do. Whether the segments have any connection with market reality is another matter. One of the implications of Ehrenberg's findings is that in many product fields, segments do not appear to exist in the way that marketers fondly believe. The danger of complex techniques is that we believe the results just because we do not understand them – they look impressive.

When we take the first two problems together, we get the group of techniques that measure wrong concepts. We saw that so-called hierarchical models of consumer buying (awareness, interest, belief, etc) have no basis in fact. But the various stages are easy to measure, so researchers produce numbers on awareness, brand recall and so on at the drop of a hat. They have no relationship with market behaviour at all, and such measurements should be used only as a comforter.

Market research is reactive

A more general criticism of the use of market research in branding is that it is necessarily *reactive*: it can only measure responses to what is past or to what is hypothetically asked of respondents. One view is that, in competitive markets, all the major firms are doing the same market research, coming up with the same answers, and producing very similar brands. What is needed instead is the real creative leap forward, the breakthrough. The problem is that the more innovative the idea, the more difficult it is for consumers to respond to it sensibly.

The extreme reaction to such problems is to say that market research is of no use at all, particularly with new products. This is said to be the Japanese approach: the only thing to do is to get the product out on to the market and see if people buy it. In fact, the major Japanese companies do have thorough basic market research at their fingertips. They also have the priceless advantage not found in most Western countries, of a docile and biddable retail channel that will accept a stream of new brands. (See the earlier example of 1,000 new soft drinks in a year.) Some entrepreneurs do not believe in doing market research (eg Richard Branson); they rely on their instinct or gut feel, and that is what makes them successful, but unfortunately most of us are not like that.

For most firms, some marketing information is essential. With all the attendant problems, what information do they need and how should they set about getting it?

What information do we need?

At the basic level, what we need to know about our markets is the answers to the questions 'who', 'what', 'when', 'where', perhaps 'how' and, if possible, 'why'. Who buys, who else is involved, who influences? What brand, what variety (size, flavour, etc), how much, what price was paid? When during the buying cycle (year, month, week), how often? At which store or outlet, through which media (phone, fax, Internet)? What was the decision process, what other products or brands were considered, what information was collected? What was the motivation?

You will see that the first four questions can receive factual answers, because they measure behaviour. The last two begin to stray into the tricky territory discussed above. That is why the basic data should concentrate on behaviour, on what can be measured reliably. In fmcg markets, such data are commonplace, and are usually available from many suppliers either as part of a syndicated service or produced specially. Obviously, all information has a cost, and even in large fmcg fields companies do not collect all the data every year.

In Britain, a regular survey of behaviour is called a 'Usage and Attitude Study' (or U&A); in the United States it is known as an 'A&U' (for Awareness and Usage). This, together with any regular measures such as panel surveys (which measure buying patterns or retail sales) or, increasingly, data from scanning systems, forms the basis of the brand information system.

In business-to-business markets and emerging services fields such surveys are not so common. However, the basic U&A study can be carried out in any market, and should be considered by any company that does not have any basic market information. Given the importance of trial and repeat purchase in forming brand share, these should be measured as accurately as possible. They are the fundamental mechanics of a market, and must be understood if realistic plans for a brand are to be made. In some fields there may be difficulties in such measurement – and indeed in certain markets they may not be applicable – but some attempt is recommended.

Even more fundamentally, in my view firms need to understand the *product in use*. This means going beyond buying data to see how the brand fits into the buyer's and user's life. When do they use it exactly, how, in what context? What problems are they trying to solve, what are the constraints? What other products form part of the context, what is their relationship to our brand?

It is only through this sort of approach that you will begin to reach real empathy with your consumers, and to see how you need to develop your brand to offer the benefits people really want. Such research will be at least partly qualitative, and is discussed below.

Beyond these basic data, what do we need? Obviously, we need to obtain some feel for those aspects that make the *brand* different from the product.

Branding research

If we know relatively little about our market, or about the product in use, or about the nature of our brand, we need to start with *qualitative* research. As the name suggests, this does not produce numbers, but explores how consumers talk about the product field, what concepts and words they use, how they feel. It should be used to develop *hypotheses* for further testing, but should never be used as if it produced reliable measures based on a representative sample.

Unfortunately, qualitative research is fairly cheap, and produces rich and fascinating quotes from real consumers, so it is a temptation to rely on it too much. 'One wonders how many marketing pipe dreams and wasted marketing resources are generated each year on the basis of such endorsements as, "It was gangbusters in the focused group sessions" ' (Weilbacher, 1993, p 140).

In particular, in developing branding we need to start with soft data, with feelings. Remembering the scepticism expressed above about attitude and motivational research, we still need to use *some* means of exploring behaviour in great depth, and of going beyond behaviour. For this we need in-depth interviews or group discussions.

Leo Burnett, the great advertising practitioner and founder of the international agency, was a great believer in carrying out personal interviews himself to get a feel for his target audience.

One Japanese company sends out their senior executives with a local consultant to spend up to two hours or more in people's homes, asking – and observing – in great detail about every aspect of their use of electronic appliances. Such research can be carried out only on a small scale, but it can produce results of enormous richness, full of insights and suggestions. It should form part of every firm's branding process.

Group discussions (or 'focus groups') and some of their attendant problems were mentioned above. Despite the dangers, they can be used sensibly to produce important qualitative data, and indeed are often the essential starting point for brand development.

To get behind the rational, conscious responses to the deeper layers beneath, a range of techniques can be used. *Projective techniques*, borrowed from psychology, give respondents exercises in which they 'project' their unconscious feelings about products and brands. An example is:

You are at a party, and the brands come through the door.
Describe the person each brand would be.
If this brand were an animal, what would it be?
If this brand were a car, what would it be?
Draw a picture (or tell a story) about this brand.

The techniques should explore the explicit and dormant brand values, and the *relationship* between consumer and brand – for example, by asking not only what respondents think about the brand, but also 'What does the brand think about you?' Some people may find such suggestions fanciful, but the reality is that consumers can and do describe the personality of well-known brands, and such techniques are essential in teasing out brand values – always, of course, with the caveat entered above about the readiness of respondents to answer *any* question, however irrelevant to their real experience.

Another technique is the *repertory grid*, in which respondents are asked to sort brands into groups and explain what distinguishes the groups. This will extract a series of concepts that can form the basis of attitude scales for further quantitative testing.

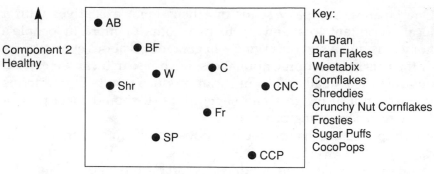

A perceptual map produced for the cereal market on two principal components. The two components are weighted averages of attributes monitored in the survey. Examining the attributes which make up the components suggests appropriate descriptive labels, as shown.

Source: Corstjens (1990)

Figure 4.2 *Example of a brand map*

It is this *quantitative* stage that ought to be the next stage. We cannot rely on the results of a small sample in qualitative studies, and need a properly designed survey on a large sample. Only in this way can we be confident how our target market thinks and feels about our brand. Firms also typically use the quantitative stage to explore possible segments, and to produce brand maps. Details of such techniques are beyond the scope of this book, but an example of a brand map is shown in Figure 4.2.

How some of the results from branding research are used in brand planning is discussed in the next chapter.

5

Brand Stretching and Brand Extensions

In earlier chapters we saw that on the one hand strong brands are extremely valuable properties, and on the other that meaningless extensions and over-proliferation can be serious threats to a brand's future.

This dilemma is at the centre of brand management: how far can we stretch the brand so as to make the most of its strength, but at the same time protect the core values of the brand in the face of extensions further and further away from its basic identity?

Consider the following examples:

- Mitsubishi stretches from heavy industry through cars to banking, electronics and even food.
- Virgin publishes music, runs an airline, and sells vodka, cola and financial services.
- Levi's Tailored Classics clothes were a failure, despite the enormous strength of the parent brand.
- Bic perfume failed.
- Caterpillar boots – that is, from heavy earth-moving equipment to fashion clothing – were a success!

The temptation to capitalize on success, to maximize the value of a strong brand, is huge. To build a major new consumer brand in the three main market areas (the United States, Japan and Europe) is estimated to cost up to US $1 billion, but to launch a new product under the name of an established brand will cost a fraction of that. Moreover, there is a belief that brand extensions have more chance of success than completely new brands. The evidence is unclear.

One study showed that only 30 per cent of new brands survive more than three years, but when they are launched under the name of an existing brand, the survival rate is 50 per cent (Kapferer, 1992, p 84). Another study, by Nielsen, looked at 114 cases of new product launches. After two years, the products launched under their own name gained twice the share of the market compared with new products launched under the name of an existing brand (Kapferer, 1992, p 105). Yet another study found that, of fmcg products introduced into US supermarkets over a period of 10 years, fully two thirds of those that were successful (ie sales over US $15 million) were line extensions rather than new brands (quoted in Arnold, 1992, p 142).

One explanation for these results could be that truly innovative new products, which gain a significant share, do better as completely new brands. Small improvements are more likely to succeed under an established name, though they will gain only modest market shares. Brand extensions, on this argument, are safe and cheap – but they will not set the world on fire.

Small wonder, then, that in these days when managers are expected to 'make assets sweat' – and when there is a premium on apparent efficiency rather than risk-taking – there is pressure to stretch brands as far as they will go.

Although the categories overlap, and the terms 'stretching' and 'extension' are often used interchangeably, we will distinguish between *stretching* a brand into new product fields and *extending* a brand by adding product variants or new products in essentially the same field.

Both types of extensions can either help the parent brand, harm the parent brand or be neutral.

As an example of the first situation, the launch of ready-to-drink Ribena in small cartons widely distributed to reach children was not only a success in its own right, but revived the previously flagging sales of the parent brand.

As to the second situation, both Pierre Cardin and Gucci undoubtedly weakened their parent brand position as luxury, *haute couture* identities by proliferation of hundreds, even thousands of products. Probably most extensions that succeed, however, are neutral in their effect.

In the rest of the chapter, we will try to find some guidance on how to avoid the worst errors, and to make the most positive contribution from using existing brands.

BRAND STRETCHING

We have already quoted examples to show that brands can be stretched over wide and disparate fields. We should start by separating out those companies whose operations cover different product fields, but where buyers do not rely on the brand's reputation in those other fields when making a purchase.

General Electric or 'GE' (the US corporation, not the British one) operates in aircraft engines, broadcasting, defence electronics, electric motors, factory automation, lighting, locomotives, domestic appliances, diagnostic imaging and financial services. Although there may be connections between some of these, in most cases a buyer of GE lighting does not have in mind the corporation's reputation in locomotives or financial services. Similarly, a buyer of a Mitsubishi car does not think of the brand as carrying over desirable qualities from its banking or shipbuilding operations. Buyers may, however, have a general view of GE or Mitsubishi as big firms with certain characteristics. (We shall return to the issue of companies as brands in Chapter 10.)

In these cases, the firm needs to establish its brand in each market separately. It might, in theory, be regarded as a collection of separate brands that happen to have the same name (the counter-arguments to this are dealt with in Chapter 10). Of more interest are those companies that deliberately try to use the reputation of the existing brand in the new market, as Levi's did in clothing and Bic in perfume. Both failed, but the idea has been used by others with great success, most notably by Virgin.

The Virgin magic

Virgin started out as a product – a publisher and retailer of popular music. Its brand was built up on the qualities expressed by its products, and the Virgin brand is now so powerful that it can be applied to fields as different as an airline, a cola and a financial service (ie a Personal Equity Plan).

The personality of the Virgin brand could be described as 'the people's brand' or 'the small firm that challenges the big bad guys who are ripping you off'. Richard Branson, the founder, sees the core values as *innovation*, *quality* and *fun*.

Virgin or Branson?

Virgin is so inextricably bound up with the public persona of Richard Branson that some people question which actually is the brand. Some extraordinary results of a survey (*PR Week*, 9 September 1994) throw some light on this:

■ Branson is known by 97 per cent of the population, Virgin by 93 per cent.

■ Branson's personal image scores extremely high, with 92 per cent describing him as 'clever', 86 per cent as 'likeable' and 71 per cent as 'trustworthy'.

■ A remarkable 34 per cent say that they would be more likely to buy a Virgin product or service because of their opinion of Branson.

■ Virgin is seen as 'friendly' (83 per cent), 'high quality' (75 per cent), 'fun' (68 per cent) and 'innovative' (66 per cent).

Interestingly, the great mass of the people – that is, the market – see both Branson and Virgin in very positive terms. The criticism that Branson is an egotistic publicity-seeker is not what most people think. He personifies the brand, and the public likes the personality. Even his sometimes boyish pranks are part of this personality, and reflect the 'against the establishment' flavour of the brand. Of course, the sheer value of the huge press coverage is extremely effective too! As Jeremy Bullmore said (see Chapter 1), all great brands have a sort of fame – and Virgin/Branson have certainly achieved that.

How far can Virgin go?

There are two related questions about the Virgin brand in the future: how far can it be stretched, and what will it be without Branson? As to the first, he himself has said (in a private conversation with the author) that the brand can be applied to 'anything, as long as it's high quality'.

While some may be sceptical about this, we must all admit that we might have been sceptical when we first heard of a Virgin airline. This did not, on the face of it, build squarely on the existing brand franchise. To succeed, it needed to appeal to a new segment of hard-headed business travellers as well as to the young back-packers in the economy section. Yet it has been a success.

Virgin is constantly bombarded by proposals for products to be branded as Virgin, and it turns most of them down. Branson and his colleagues have a clear idea of what the brand stands for, and a shrewd commercial instinct for markets in which they can make a real difference. Their venture into railways has been less successful. As many of the companies that took over the privatized railways found out, running a train service is a lot harder than it looks from the outside. Virgin Trains have had a great deal of bad publicity as a result of faults in their train services. Even if they get it right eventually – and Branson himself remains confident – the question remains as to what damage the poor service may do to the core brand (a question we return to in Chapter 10).

The further question, as to what will happen when Branson himself is no longer around, is more difficult. He himself is confi-dent that the team in place can carry on successfully, as the ethos is strongly established. What they are certain to miss is his flair for publicity and his entrepreneurial sense. As for strategy, Virgin has a similar problem to that of Club Med – that the original buyers are getting older. Being too closely identified with one young age generation can be dangerous, and the stronger the brand image, the more likely it is that the succeeding generations will reject the brand as 'not for us' – as the 'Pepsi generation' have been encour-aged to reject Coke. Both Virgin and Club Med have coped successfully with this so far by modifying their product range and offering new services, but it will be a constant challenge.

What can we learn from these different experiences of success and failure? There must be some general factors that support brand stretching, and some that work against it.

Factors supporting stretch

No single factor by itself will guarantee success, but there do seem to be certain common characteristics. As with all business 'rules', there will also be exceptions to many.

Awareness and reputation of parent
As Virgin shows, a brand with very high public awareness and a good reputation starts with an advantage. The Levi's experience demonstrates that this on its own is not enough: although the brand has very high awareness, its reputation for blue jeans did not transfer to formal clothing.

Is the brand essence still applicable?
Bic's brand essence and its core values are about the mass production of small pieces of metal and plastic equipment at low prices. This can be extended from disposable pens to disposable lighters, but not to perfume. Levi's are known for rugged jeans expressing the 'old frontier' values of independence and informality; these are not relevant in more formal clothing. The Bill Blass name in the United States carries connotations of prestige, couture clothing, but it did not work when applied to chocolates. Both Caterpillar and Jeep, on the other hand, were able to apply their brand essences ('tough', 'outdoor', 'workmanlike') to fashion shoes – because, at the time anyway, those values also characterized what people were looking for in leisure clothing.

Expertise and know-how transferability
Apart from the core values, it seems that the brand must be *believable* in its new field. You would believe that Sony could make any electronic appliance to a high standard – this is being tested at present as they try to extend the brand to personal computers. Of course, this is one rule that Virgin has bent, at the very least. It could hardly be argued that its previous competences equipped it to run an airline. Perhaps its reputation for quality outweighed its lack of engineering or operational expertise in any related field.

Perceived difficulty of manufacture
The extent of transferability of expertise is connected to how difficult consumers perceive the manufacture of the new product to be or the new service to provide. If it is seen to be easy, a strong brand will have relatively less of an advantage. Where it is thought to be difficult, a strong existing brand will transfer much more of its influence. This is a reflection of our reaction to uncertainty: the more uncertainty or risk there is in buying or

using a product, the more we should prefer to rely on a well-known name. Sony may have had more of an advantage some years ago in entering the personal computer market because, at that time, computers were seen as complicated, hi-tech machines. Now, as they are made by hundreds of firms, Sony's name is probably worth rather less.

How comfortable is the new brand beside the old?

This is more formally known as 'complementarity' or 'fit'. Vodka and cola fit quite comfortably with records for Virgin, because they are all products bought by the same consumer segment, and can share Virgin's brand values. The various Dunhill products – smoking articles, clothing, fragrances – all fit quite comfortably together under the upmarket prestige brand. As a generalization, it may be that prestige or other emotional values are more transferable than functional ones (Aaker, 1991, p 220).

A real market gap exists

This should go without saying, but it is still true: a gap must exist, not just for the new product, but *for the product branded with this particular brand*. There may be a gap for a Dunhill blazer, but not for a Levi's blazer. Researching the concept with target consumers may help to identify potential winners and losers. However, sometimes only a real test in the market place will show what people will buy.

Factors operating against stretch

In general, we can say that these are the opposite or absence of the factors working in favour of stretch, that is, those we have just looked at. More specifically, we can list the following mistakes to avoid.

Inappropriate associations

Levi's and Bic perfumes have been quoted several times. Again, research should be able to identify the existing brand associations, and what consumers feel would be appropriate and inappropriate extensions. The associations of Caterpillar with heavy machinery can be extended to a work-boot style of footwear but, as for Levi's, would probably be inappropriate for more formal styles.

Wrong associations
Campbell's launched Prego spaghetti sauces, but they failed. The associations of Campbell's soup were 'orange' and 'watery', and did not carry over to the new product – even though its soups were very successful. Arm & Hammer successfully extended its values associated with getting rid of smells from baking soda to oven cleaner, but could not do so for underarm deodorant; presumably the thought of putting something associated with the power of oven cleaner on a tender part of your body is not attractive.

Unbelievable claims
Amstrad was a British manufacturer of consumer electrical and electronic products, well-known for offering value-for-money products at the bottom end of the price range. Therefore, Amstrad prestige cars, for example, would not be a believable proposition.

BRAND EXTENSIONS

By 'brand extension' we mean the introduction of a new product using the existing brand name in the same or a closely related field. It is often called 'line extension', and forms a major part of the marketing activity of many fmcg companies. One study found that almost nine out of ten so-called new product introductions were in fact line extensions (Aaker, 1991, p 208). The results of this proliferation were discussed in Chapter 3 above.

There are, of course, good reasons for the prevalence of line extensions:

■ You can capitalize on the value of the brand you have spent so much on building up.
■ It is cheaper than launching a free-standing brand.
■ It is more likely to succeed.
■ It may revitalize the parent brand – as ready-diluted Ribena in one-drink ambient packaging did.
■ You may want to forestall competitors by filling a niche, or you may have to match their actions.
■ Either the changing market, or emerging technology, may offer the opportunity for a new variant.
■ There may be a gap in your product line, which either customers or consumers would like to see filled.

■ Your line extension may take shelf space which otherwise would be available to your competitors.

All these *can* be perfectly sound reasons for extending brands. The major reason must be to produce greater long-term profit, though unfortunately it often seems that the real motivation is to show higher short-term sales. The two may be compatible, but there are dangers in thoughtless extensions that may work against the long-term health of the brand.

Weakening the parent brand

If you have a strong parent brand, the absolute priority must be to nurture and defend it. Extensions may help to do that, but they may also weaken it in four ways:

■ Extensions that fail may damage consumers' faith in the parent.
■ The extensions may merely take sales away from the parent ('cannibalization'), leaving it weaker.
■ Both managerial time and the total budget will be split between the original brand and the new lines. The single-minded concentration of managers and the strategic concentration of force that previously supported the parent brand will no longer be there.
■ Retailers have only limited space, and every additional line makes additional demands. They may be reluctant to accept all extensions, or they may just allocate the extension some space from your existing allowance – automatically reducing that given to the main brand.

In today's complex and dynamic markets, there are no 'right' answers to these dilemmas. One view is that even Coca-Cola has gone too far. For most of its long and successful life, Coca-Cola was a single-product brand. Even new pack sizes were introduced reluctantly and in reaction to competitive brands. Eventually it decided – again apparently in response to competitors – to extend. You can now buy Classic Coke, Diet Coke, Cherry Coke, Caffeine-free Coke, Caffeine-free Diet Coke and so on. Some critics argue that this will in the long run confuse consumers, and weaken the franchise of one of the world's great brands. Only time will tell.

Some of the guidelines for deciding whether and how to extend a brand are essentially the same as those for stretching it into new fields. Others, such as those to do with technical expertise, are clearly less relevant here.

As an example of how one firm tries to maintain the integrity of the brand, there follows a statement about Oreos, those chocolate sandwich cookies with a creme filling that are a central feature of the American way of life. The communications of the extension are guided by a statement of beliefs about the brand.

> We allow ourselves to alter the size of the cookie as long as it is round. We can vary the amount of creme in the center. We can change the colour of the creme as long as it tastes the same. We can use different outside coatings for the cookie. And finally, we can play with the size and shape of the package as long as the trademark is consistent...
>
> We have a very clear and comprehensive understanding of the brand's consumer image. Oreo is fun and playful, it is never serious or somber. Oreo is irresistibly delicious. Oreo is part of living. It is as American as apple pie. Oreo is loved by the whole family. It is truly for the kid in all of us, which encompasses all age groups. And Oreo evokes rich associations of family, friends, youth and indulgence.
>
> (John Greeniaus, quoted in Weilbacher, 1993, p 37)

This sort of framework does not guarantee success, but it will prevent a lot of unnecessary failures. It gives clear guidance as to what are the central values of the brand, and thus what extensions are compatible with them and what are not.

The lessons, then, are that both brand stretching and extensions can be successful and profitable – if they are done right. That means building on the brand's core values, introducing only products that fit the brand and genuinely offer the buyers value. Extensions can be valuable competitive weapons and can revive tired brands, but they can also weaken the brand if done carelessly or for the wrong reasons.

Campbell's Soup was quoted earlier as an example of proliferation. Under David Johnson, the company has shown an average annual growth in net profits of 17 per cent since 1990. According to Mr Johnson, 'There is no such thing as a mature market, only tired marketers.' Campbell's has driven volumes by adding new flavours, improving recipes, and offering 'healthy' soups with less salt and fat (*Financial Times*, 10 September 1996).

Campbell's seems to be doing it right, but others are questioning their previous policies. Unilever has announced that it will cut its 1,600 global brands to only 400, and even the mighty Procter and Gamble has reached a similar conclusion; Heinz and Diageo agree. Famous names such as Pears soap, Findus frozen food, Cinzano and Heinz salad cream are surplus to requirements (*Financial Times*, 29 October 1999). What all these fmcg giants recognize is that the result of decades of brand and product proliferation is vast over-supply. The huge number of brands means that resources are over-stretched, and the really powerful brands – on which the company's future depends – are starved of funds. Research suggests that there is far too much product duplication and clutter in today's market place. Brand stretching and line extensions are not yet obsolete, but we shall see many companies cutting back on clutter, to concentrate their forces on fewer – but bigger – global winners.

6

Advertising, Promotion and the Brand

Earlier chapters have mentioned the important role of advertising and promotion in fmcg markets. Advertising has been seen as one of the primary tools of brand building and, as Chapter 3 discussed, the high cost and difficulties of mass advertising are seen as one of the major challenges to fmcg brands. This chapter will examine what we know about how advertising and promotion actually work, and what each can and cannot do for brands.

For clarity, let us define some of the terms that will be used in this chapter, as they are easy to confuse. Readers who know the terms may skip these basic explanations.

Advertising is all paid-for persuasive communication in the main media of television, press, posters, cinema and radio – that is, what we usually mean by advertisements but excluding other forms of publicity which lay people sometimes refer to as advertising (eg sponsorship). Advertising is referred to as 'above the line' for historical reasons, as advertising agencies used to receive commission from media owners on it – and often still do. All other forms of sales promotion are called 'below the line'.

Promotion covers activities designed to increase sales by offering an inducement, such as extra product, free gifts, competitions and so on. It can be split into: 1) *trade promotion*, aimed at distributors and designed to encourage them to stock the brand, increase the space allocated to it or otherwise to try to sell more; and 2) *consumer promotion*, aimed directly at consumers and designed to encourage them to buy.

The term 'promotion' is also used loosely to cover the vast variety of ways firms try to gain publicity for and increase sales of their brands.

DO ALL BRANDS NEED ADVERTISING?

We have made the assumption that brands need advertising – but some strong brands apparently do not. Marks & Spencer used to spend almost nothing on advertising, yet it was an enormously powerful brand. The Body Shop, too, seems to have built up a distinct brand personality without heavy advertising. Of course, both these are retailers: they have stores which people pass by, and go into. The stores themselves are – in their way – advertising, and it is difficult to think of major brands other than retailers that have done without advertising. It is also true that, as Jeremy Bullmore has pointed out, 'It is extremely difficult (impossible) to adjust brand reputations without *controlled* communications – both [Marks & Spencer and The Body Shop] being examples' (1999). It is noticeable that, in late 1999 when Marks & Spencer was in serious trouble, it started to use advertising to help recover its reputation. There are niche brands that have built up a reputation by word of mouth, or by making sure that they were newsworthy. Sometimes they achieve this through public relations, as The Body Shop has in its 'public interest' campaigns against testing on animals; at other times, they achieve it just by being controversial, as Benetton has notoriously done with its advertising. As Table 6.1 shows, there are many ways in which a brand can try to become famous.

We can safely make three statements about brand communications:

■ Every brand must have some means of communicating with its buyers. This may not be advertising, but it must be direct if it is to be controllable.
■ Many other methods of communication are available, and can be used to gear up and multiply the effects of advertising.

Table 6.1 *How to create a fashion out of a product*

How to become newsworthy	How to be seen as desirable	How to get other people to create the identity for you	How to get people to try it	How to move from country of strength	How to spread the gospel of the world number one
High visibility	Opinion leaders	Legends	Sampling	Borrow national identity	Be the ambassador of the product category
Free publicity	Success to success	Endorsements	New distributor	Offer exclusive premieres to partners	Offer sneak preview to VIP audiences
International	Showcase distribution	Visible consumption	Line targeting urgent/impulsive need	Create jetsetting media/stages	Lead on quality/service commitment: global and locally
Journalists' favourite	Premium prices	Unique point of sales	Gifting vehicles		Make heroes of product's unique positive qualities
	Hard to get?	Jetsetters' word of mouth			
	Sexy?	Great photographic images			
		Great logo			

Source: Macrae *et al*, 1996, p 117

Newsworthiness and fame can be achieved, but the message has to be one that is really new and interesting.

■ All the means of communication and the messages transmitted must be co-ordinated to make sure that they are saying the same thing. Confused consumers don't buy.

WHAT CAN ADVERTISING DO?

So much money is spent on advertising, by so many bright people, that it is not surprising that theories abound as to what it does and how it does it. Sadly, most of these are based on myth and personal experience rather than hard, scientific evidence. It is tempting to adopt the advice of the famous Hollywood producer about film-making: 'What you have to remember is that nobody knows anything.'

Large, sophisticated companies – the Unilevers, Procter and Gambles and Mars of this world – have been working for decades on the problem. Many of them undoubtedly have useful models that they use in their planning; but the more useful the model, the less likely they are to tell the rest of us about it!

Any firm that really wishes to find out how advertising works *for them* must commit itself to the same sort of long-term experimentation, data collection and model-building that the leaders have. Ready-made solutions are not likely to be of more than general help.

There is, however, some hope. In recent years – and for the first time – large amounts of data have become available that allow us to make some general statements. The data are 'single source'; that is, they measure actual buying and actual media exposure on the same sample of people. This is possible through new technology including hand-held scanners, smart cards, and satellite monitoring. As is to be expected, they concentrate on fmcg products, and most results are from the United States at present. But the patterns found are stable across many markets, and based on them we may at least form hypotheses about how advertising works in other fields. These hypotheses (adapted from Ambler and Vakratsas, 1995; Jones, 1995) are summarized individually below.

Short-term advertising elasticities are low

Advertising elasticities – that is, the measure of how sales change in response to a change in advertising spend – are low. They are significant in 33 per cent of cases for established brands and 55 per cent of cases for new brands. The findings show that: 1) in two thirds of campaigns for existing brands and almost half those for new brands, the advertising does not significantly affect sales (though see below for what it may be doing); and 2) short-term advertising elasticities can be measured, but they are likely to be small – around 0.2 (an increase of 1 per cent in the advertising budget will produce an increase of 0.2 per cent in sales). We must note here that this finding is disputed by another school of thought, which claims that it is indeed possible to measure the short-term effects of advertising. The details of the argument are beyond the scope of this book, but we should keep in mind that nothing is certain in the world of advertising.

The major influences on sales are, in order of magnitude:

1. behavioural loyalty (that is, the effect of the product in use);
2. promotion, which may have an elasticity up to 20 times greater than advertising (but again, see below for what this means); and
3. advertising (and here, share of voice and relative frequency are what matters).

Advertising effects are weaker in unambiguous product fields, and stronger where products are new and/or ambiguous.

Long-term effects may or may not be sales increases

Long-term effects may last two or three years after the initial campaign, so where advertising does produce a sales effect, its profitability should be measured over that period. Even if advertising produces no sales increase, it may be contributing to the maintenance of brand share, or building up brand equity (see the Broadbent quotation in 'An integrated view is needed' below).

Competitive effects must be taken into account

This may seem obvious, but not all models of advertising effect do in fact include competitive actions. Short-term effects, which we hope will be positive but may also be negative, contribute to long-term effect – but only allowing for the relative effect of both our advertising and our rivals'. For example, our short-term gain this period may be cancelled out by competitive gains in succeeding periods if we stop advertising but the competitors do not.

Low frequency is enough

A frequency of impact of one to three per buying cycle is enough to produce an effect on sales. Indeed, some evidence suggests that the response to advertising is definitely one of diminishing returns: 75 per cent of sales come from the first exposure (Jones, 1995, p 28).

There is a price paradox

The standard model of advertising and the brand suggests that a strong brand is less sensitive to price than a weaker one. The evidence here shows that, when *advertising increases sales, the average sensitivity to price also increases*. In other words, a seemingly successful campaign has made buyers more sensitive to price, whereas we would expect our brand buyers to be, if anything, less sensitive (because they have been convinced of the benefits of the brand). This paradox needs further study. One explanation is that the campaign has attracted marginal buyers, who are less committed to the brand than the previous core.

How advertising works

Cognition, affect, and experience are the main factors that must be taken into account in understanding how advertising works. Translated, this means how we *think* about a brand, what we *feel* about it and what we *know* about it from experience must all be built into any model we develop. Leaving out one or more is likely to misrepresent reality. The relative importance of each may vary in different product–market situations, but they will all be present in every case.

The hierarchy of effects model is not supported

The widely accepted model that people move through a hierarchy of stages – ignorance, awareness, belief, conviction and purchase,

	Think	**Feel**
High involvement	Informative	Affective
Low involvement	Habitual	Satisfaction

The model divides purchases into High and Low Involvement, and the purchasing decision into whether we predominantly react to cognitive stimuli ('Think') or affective ('Feel'). For example, when we buy a high-involvement item such as a new stereo system, and make the decision mainly on rational grounds, advertising works in an Informative way.

Source: Vaughn, 1986

Figure 6.1 *FCB grid of advertising effects*

for example – is definitely not borne out by the single-source data. This means that many dimensions commonly used in measuring advertising effects – awareness, recall, advertising recall, belief and so on – are not reliable. The grid developed by FCB shown in Figure 6.1 is a much more reliable approach.

Information is not necessary to persuasion

Advertising need not be informative to work. This may be comforting to those who already believed it. It does not mean that consumers are being 'irrational', but that the other elements of affect ('how we feel') and experience ('what we know') may be at least as important.

An integrated view is needed

Advertising cannot be evaluated separately: it is an inextricable part of the total brand, and some way must be found of evaluating the whole.

These are so far the most authoritative statements that can be made about advertising. Considerable measurement difficulties remain, since economic models have been disappointing and there are problems* of cognitive bias in other approaches. Single-source measurement offers the best hope, but of course is available only for certain types of product, and in some countries. What the evidence does tell us is, on the whole, reassuring – even if some cherished myths have been destroyed.

The role of advertising in maintaining a brand's strength has been well summed up by Simon Broadbent.

> The sales of a brand are like the height at which an airplane flies. Advertising spend is like its engines; while the engines are running, everything is fine, but when the engines stop, the descent starts. The effectiveness of branding is like the aerodynamic design of the plane. Great creative, or better design, means that by spending the same money, or by using the same engines, we can take the brand or the plane higher. If we cut the spending on advertising, or stop the engines, the better brand or plane will stay up longer. But both will come down! Note that, in this analogy, advertising both creates increases in sales (gets the plane up) and is needed to maintain sales (to stay at the same height is an achievement)... The brand image is a mass of great momentum that is slow to alter direction, and often we are dealing with unquantified effects. This does not mean that they are unreal. True marketers have the instinctive and correct feeling that the brand is the most valuable property, that it will evaporate slowly unless properly supported, and that long-term effects are the main justification for the advertising investment.
>
> (Broadbent, 1989, quoted in Arnold, 1993, p 166)

An example of the dangers of cutting advertising support for apparently stable brands was dramatically shown by the experience of the UK drinks manufacturer, Clark.

> Sales of Clark's Diamond White and K ciders and Babycham dropped 40 per cent overall in July and August from their levels a year earlier, as young drinkers switched to the fashionable alcopops... One analyst said, 'Brands don't usually disappear off the face of the earth in eight weeks'... HP Bulmer, the UK's largest cider producer... had probably suffered little. Bulmer was a strong advocate of advertising to maintain its brand strength, whereas Clark was sceptical about heavy marketing.
>
> (*Financial Times*, 11 September 1996)

Perhaps Clark is less sceptical now.

WHAT CAN PROMOTION DO?

The use of below-the-line promotion has been increasing. Between 1993 and 1995, for example, the proportion of the total shopping basket bought on promotion rose from 14 per cent to 16 per cent (Nielsen, *The British Shopper*, 1996). The main types of promotion used are listed in Table 6.2.

Table 6.2 *Types of promotion between 1993 and 1995*

Type	%
Store price reduction	35
Multi-buy/multi-save	16
Additional quantity in-pack	11
Manufacturer price reduction	11
Send away offer	6
Free item	5

(Other types, including banded packs, coupons and competitions accounted for 5 per cent or less each.)

Source: Nielsen Homescan

As casual observation will confirm, promotion is pervasive. To take coupons alone – which as we saw are one of the minor forms in overall effect – there are over 4 billion coupons distributed every year in Britain – with an astounding 8 billion plus in the peak year of 1991. What is all this activity achieving? From the same sources quoted above on advertising, we can say some important things about the effects of promotion.

Promotion works very well in increasing sales short-term

The elasticity of sales to promotion is up to 20 times that of advertising. This does not mean that every promotion will necessarily be hugely successful, but that a well-chosen, well-run promotion ought to produce immediate effects.

But the effects are short-term

The effects of a promotion may not last beyond the buying cycle. Moreover, the next cycle may see a corresponding *drop* in sales, as some buyers who bought with the promotion were just stocking up.

And may therefore be unprofitable

All promotions cost money, not just for the actual promotion itself, but for all the disruption in production schedules, distribution and so forth that is necessarily also involved. If the total effect on sales – however impressive the short-term gain – is neutral, then overall profit has not gone up.

> Indeed, it seems clear that in most circumstances, manufacturers that promote heavily are deliberately exchanging profit for volume: in other words, making less profit on more sales; or, to make the point more crudely, slicing into their own margins in dumping their merchandise.
>
> (Jones, 1990)

This is particularly true for the most effective promotions – that is, price reductions.

Other effects

Like advertising, promotion can do more things than just affect sales. First, it can induce consumers to try a product; because trial is hugely important in producing market share, anything that increases it is invaluable. A successful promotion that induces new triers to buy is therefore a vital weapon. It is then up to the performance of the product itself – and the subsequent actions of the rest of the marketing mix – to persuade that buyer to continue buying.

Promotion can also create excitement. In any crowded market place, you need to stand out. One way of doing this apart from advertising is having occasional creative promotions. You will all have your favourites (and pet hates); famous promotions such as the Esso tiger tails or Persil rail tickets were enormously successful in creating interest as well as sales. Unfortunately, not all excitement is good, as Hoover found out with their disastrously misjudged air ticket scheme, which must have generated more *bad* publicity than any other in recent decades.

Finally, promotion can produce a trade push: if advertising produces consumer *pull*, the trade promotion ought to produce channel *push*, ie pushing products into the distribution chain, and relying on the channel members to sell them on. So it can, but all too often it is merely the reflection of retailer power. The customer *demands* trade promotions, or at least promotional funds. Many manufacturers suspect that such funds go more or less straight to the retailer's bottom line, and have little or no effect on the effort put behind the brand. (The effect of retailer power is discussed in more depth in the next chapter.) Competitive pressures may mean that it is extremely difficult to resist the customer's demands, but evidence suggests that most trade promotions are unprofitable to the manufacturer.

There is a potentially much more deadly long-term effect of too much promotion – the subconscious message that constant promotion sends to consumers: *'Our brand isn't valuable enough on its own merits for you to buy all the time, so here is an irrelevant inducement to persuade you.'* Constant promotion must devalue the brand, sending almost the opposite message to the one you want to send.

Ideally, you want to create a brand that offers buyers superior value – and allows you to charge a premium price. The value must be central to the brand, not reproducible by rivals or own labels. Promotions are easy to imitate, and can lead to a self-destructive cycle of escalation; the newspaper wars in Britain provide a gruesome example. Most mass-market newspapers have become locked into a cycle of competitive promotions that leaves no one a winner. Profits must be damaged in the short term. In the longer term, the real danger is that constant promotion will turn the product category into a commodity with no differentiation and fierce price competition.

INTEGRATING ADVERTISING AND PROMOTION

The answer to the problem of conflicting communications must be to *integrate* advertising and promotion, what the Americans call – as if it were something new – 'Integrated Marketing Communications'. There are two common sense reasons for integration.

The first reason is that integration creates synergy. This is a much-abused word, but the evidence shows clearly that advertising and promotion can work together to produce a greater effect. The average advertising elasticity is around 0.2, but when run jointly with promotion it goes up to 1.6 – that is, eight times the effect (Jones, 1995, p 28).

In addition, the integration of advertising and promotion gives the consumer a coherent message. The point has been made before, and will be again, since it is so fundamental but so often ignored: *all elements of the marketing mix must work together to give the same message.* If advertising and promotion are to achieve synergy and to build a cumulative effect in consumers' minds, they must be mutually consistent. All managers probably start out this way, but it seems that during the year new opportunities arise – 'the chance to get in on an exciting new development', 'an unrepeatable special offer' – or old constraints (such as budget cuts), so coherence goes out of the window. Look carefully at all the advertising and promotion campaigns you can, and see how many of them demonstrate real, coherent targeting of a consistent message.

PLANNING ADVERTISING AND PROMOTION

It follows that we need to plan. There is not room here to go into all the detail necessary for proper planning of an advertising and promotion campaign, but let us at least look at a framework.

Obviously, the advertising and promotion plan is only one part of the overall marketing plan, and must fit within it. In order to start the advertising plan, then, we need some background. Note that this is not a plea for very formal, restrictive planning, but for a process of *thinking through* what the advertising and promotion are trying to achieve.

From the brand plan (see Chapter 12 below) we should expect to find the following elements:

▓ a situation analysis (where we are and why);
▓ objectives (what the brand is aiming for in sales, share and other targets);
▓ positioning (how the brand is positioned in the consumer's mind, and how we wish to change this);

▓ strategy (how the brand is going to compete in this market);
▓ advertising strategy (what role advertising has next period within the overall strategy); and
▓ budget (what moneys are available to spend on advertising and promotion).

The question of budget is of course a knotty one, and much argued over. As we have seen, advertising is thought to be an essential tool in brand building, but its effects – particularly in the short term, ie this year – are difficult or impossible to measure. Making a case for a large sum is not easy.

Deciding on the size of appropriation is usually done in one of two ways. The first method is referred to as *advertising to sales ratio*. This is probably the most common approach, even though it is strictly illogical. Using a fixed ratio to decide on the advertising budget suggests that sales cause advertising – but surely advertising causes sales? Despite this, ratios are used – and are at least simple.

The second method for deciding on the size of appropriation is *share of voice*. This is also known as 'competitive parity', and rightly suggests that the budget is set according to our relative share of the market. If we are aiming to expand our share, then we assume that we have to increase our share of voice too. As a corollary, the market leader ought to be able to get away with spending *less* than its strict share of voice while still maintaining share.

Neither of these is very scientific, but as the earlier discussion showed, a committed effort in model building over many years is needed to produce a better method. It is easy to say that this should be the aim of all brand builders, but for many firms in many markets that must be a pious hope.

Another method of setting budgets is known as *objective and task*. It uses the hierarchy of effects approach, setting targets for awareness, knowledge, liking, preference and so on. The evidence quoted earlier showed that this hierarchy is not a reliable model, therefore *the objective and task method is not reliable either*. This is a harsh judgment, but one fully justified by our current knowledge. The reason that such intermediate objectives are used so often is that it is difficult to brief an advertising agency to, for example, increase brand share by two percentage points. They need to be told what the advertising is expected to achieve, and that means communications objectives.

Given what we do know, advertising objectives must include long-term brand building. They may of course also include shorter-term tasks such as announcing a new variation or promotion.

The size of the budget is only one of the decisions to be made. Other important decisions have to do with media, content and creative treatment. To some extent they all interact, and you can start from anywhere. You may have a particularly exciting creative treatment that demands a particular medium. Alternatively, you may start with the content and go on to the creative treatment, which suggests a specific budget level. In other cases, competitive arguments may force you to choose a medium – 'We must be on television, because they are' – which then calls for particular content and treatment. The decisions cannot be made in isolation, but must always be seen in the context of the overall marketing plan.

Promotions, as we have argued above, should be integrated into this process. Bad practice finds 'consumer promotion £x,000 in cycle 6' without further elaboration. These are the cases that produce reactive, irrelevant promotions that may harm the brand. Good practice sees the objectives of promotions set at the beginning and in the context of the communications strategy, so that suitable, relevant promotions consistent with the brand's values can be planned. Promotions agencies are very good at coming up with ideas, as are advertising agencies, but the ideas must contribute to, and express, the brand's values.

RELATIONSHIP, ONE-TO-ONE AND DIRECT MARKETING

So far we have talked as if advertising and promotion in the traditional sense were all that there is. In recent years, however, new ways of communicating with consumers – or adaptations of old ways – have appeared. In this so-called 'new marketing', what is important is not just the one good hit that converts a buyer for this one occasion, but the relationship with each buyer over many years. New means of communicating are wanted – and exist.

What suppliers of consumer goods have realized is what people in industrial or business-to-business markets have already known for a long time: the lifetime value of a buyer is huge compared with the value of one purchase. Since it may cost up to 10 times as much to gain a new buyer as to retain an existing one, it becomes imperative to focus on the *relationship* with customers over time – and this implies communicating with them as individuals, not as a homogeneous mass.

New technology, specifically that of computing, allows this to be done. The foundations of the direct or one-to-one marketing approach that has emerged as a result of this new technology are: a database of clients and potential customers; records for each customer and prospect which show not only all relevant classification data such as name, address and demographics, but also responses to previous communications, and – most importantly – what exactly was bought, when, at what price, in response to what offer or communication; and analysis methods that allow managers to interrogate the database, and that can identify patterns of behaviour right down to the individual level.

These methods are now extremely sophisticated, and give firms the ability to target individuals and groups of individuals accurately. Further, the firm can *measure* the effect of particular campaigns precisely, thereby allowing even greater accuracy in the next round.

It is not surprising, then, that direct marketing has made great strides in business-to-business markets, and in traditional direct selling fields such as direct mail and catalogue selling. More unexpected is the fact that many of our largest and most sophisticated fmcg companies are also experimenting with it. Firms such as Procter and Gamble, Heinz and Unilever have built up lists of consumers containing *millions* of names. They use the analysis and targeting methods described above to send information and offers to consumers, and can tailor the offer more and more closely to an individual's known preferences.

The question most relevant here is, just what effect does this have on the brand? Traditionally, theme advertising was the means by which brand image was built up. Core values, it was believed, could be transmitted only by heavy, mass advertising over time. Is this model now out of date?

It is too early to tell. The consumer-oriented direct marketing efforts are still fairly new, and the companies concerned are not giving out any results. They seem very happy with some of what they are achieving, but critics wonder about the costs and the effectiveness. The worry is that the nature of the medium used – mainly direct mail, and increasingly the Internet – may smack too much of the cheap (if not nasty), and that it may lend itself too readily to coupons and price offers. Too frequent use of such promotion, we argued earlier, will detract from the brand's core values and will inflict long-term harm.

TWO-WAY COMMUNICATION

What is encouraging about the use of new methods is that it shows that companies now recognize that they have a relationship with their buyers and users, and that they need to work at it. Communication with consumers need not be only through mass media, and it can also be a two-way process – as the increasing adoption of free telephone services shows.

The newest of the new media is of course the Internet. Growth in usership has been explosive, matched only by the extraordinary hype. Many companies have Web sites, and an increasing number of advertisements in the main media contain an Internet address. Advocates see the Web as the future – all other means of communication are out of date, obsolete.

The Internet does offer new opportunities, in particular in the fact that it is global and instant. Any individual with access, anywhere in the world, at any time of day or night, can contact the Web site, read copy, look at pictures – even moving pictures, with sound. And more important – in theory, they can *respond*. The possibilities are limitless – again, in theory. Even with wider access, how many people really want to be interactive? For what sort of products? How often? (Chapter 14 will look at this vital topic in more detail.)

For some firms, especially in business-to-business markets, the Internet offers companies the opportunity to gain real advantage by giving their customers a real benefit. Federal Express customers, for example, can track the progress of their parcels on-line through the FedEx Web site. For many of the other sites, we can say only that there are some interesting, exciting things going on – and some pretty boring ones too. Try it and see.

What we must always remember is that these new methods must be integrated with the overall brand plan if they are to be both efficient and effective. The overriding purpose of communicating brand values to customers and consumers must stay at the forefront of managers' minds, through all the dazzle and hype of new technology.

7

The Role of Retailers

Virtually all fmcg brands use retailers, as do most consumer durables and many services. For all these, the role of the distributor – once thought of as passive, merely a channel – has become more and more important. If your product or service does not use retailers and never will, you may wish to skip this chapter.

For everyone else, retailers present new challenges that are central to the successful brand–consumer relationship. The final, critical moment of purchase takes place at a time and in a place that is beyond the brand owner's direct control.

The problems and opportunities of supplier–retailer links are shown in the extreme form in grocery products, and much of the discussion that follows will focus on that situation. The issues, though, are fast becoming common to other fields as well. The development that has produced dramatic changes in what marketers can and cannot do with their brands is retail concentration.

CONCENTRATION AND THE POWER OF THE MULTIPLES

Retailing has been one of the most dynamic sectors in western countries during the last two decades – not in overall growth, but in innovation, efficiency and rate of change. There have been huge success stories such as Wal-Mart in the United States, and some bumpier rides such as Next. The face of our shopping streets has changed, and new shopping centres and experiences have appeared. Many of these developments reflect changes in society such as increasing wealth, widespread possession of refrigerators and freezers, vastly higher car ownership and therefore mobility, increase in the proportion of working women and much higher penetration of foreign travel. Successful retailers have taken full advantage of the new opportunities these changes have offered (see Seth and Randall, 1999).

The most visible change has been in the dramatic fall in the total number of shops, and the corresponding rise in the power of the multiple chains that have gained share. In the UK, four chains – Tesco, Sainsbury's, Asda and Safeway – had reached a dominating 60 per cent share of the total grocery market by 1995. In many other countries – Australia, Switzerland, the Scandinavian countries, Canada – the top 10 firms account for 80 per cent or more. In other fields – shoes, clothing, DIY, drugstores, electrical and electronic goods – we can see the same pattern. Only in countries such as Italy or Japan, where planning control prevents it, has concentration not progressed.

For the future, one study defined the following trends in retailing:

■ more concentration;
■ more internationalization;
■ better management;
■ more battles for share;
■ more marketing orientation;
■ more data sophistication;
■ more specialist chains;
■ more channel power;
■ more demands on suppliers;
■ new user needs;
■ new ways of shopping; and
■ shorter shop life cycles.

Some of these are key for brand builders, and we will return to them.

THE EFFECTS OF RETAIL CONCENTRATION

The new retailers have common characteristics that are particularly relevant for their suppliers. Compared with retailers in the past, they have more power, more sophisticated management, more marketing orientation, more centralized decision-making and much more data, much better used.

The first factor – and the one that has had the most dramatic impact – is *power*. In what many marketing people see as the good old days, manufacturers decided on their marketing plans and told the retailers what they were expected to do. The supplier decided on pricing, promotion and to some extent even display; the retailer was just the place consumers went to find the brands that the manufacturers' advertising had persuaded them to buy.

No longer. The multiple retailer now dominates the relationship. As the buyer is supposed to have said to the hapless representative, *'I account for 15 per cent of your sales, you account for 5 per cent of mine. Now let's talk terms.'* The manufacturer now has to negotiate – and sometimes actually pay for – space on the shelves. The retailer decides on pricing, on display and on what promotion will be accepted. The effects on brands may be that:

■ margins are under pressure;
■ advertising is cut;
■ short-term promotion and unprofitable trade promotions increase;
■ shelf space is limited;
■ brand extensions and new brands find it hard to get distribution; and
■ retailers' brands increase their share.

All this means that there is less to reinvest in new product development and brand support, so that in the medium term brands decline and die.

The change in the balance of power has led to conflict not just over margins, but also over practically every other aspect of the relationship. Often, the main attributes visible seem to be mistrust and lack of communication. More worryingly, some retailers are asking a more fundamental question.

WHO CONTROLS THE MARKETING PROCESS?

Any manufacturer producing brands thinks it alone controls the marketing process. Retailers, on the other hand, argue that they now have much better knowledge of the consumer and can put products on the shelves more efficiently than a branded manufacturer, so they should control the marketing. What, in the final analysis, does each bring to the party? The manufacturer carries out detailed market research into his markets, pays for extensive consumer advertising and develops *branding*. He provides unique consumer knowledge, and understanding of the market as a whole. The retailer collects detailed scanning data, and thus has precise feedback on *buying patterns* and the *effects of marketing action*. He knows in rich detail the minutiae of consumer shopping habits.

Retailers genuinely do have unrivalled access to tremendously detailed data on sales. They can measure exactly the effect of shelf space, location in the store, price, promotion and so on. Manufacturers, even though they can buy aggregated scanning data, can never match this level of detail. On the other hand, the retailer cannot have a deep and sympathetic understanding of every product category, whereas the manufacturer must know his particular market better than any single retailer.

Clearly, then, the two must work together. We shall return later in this chapter to how they might do this, but first we must look at two other aspects of branding: the retailer as a brand and the role of own label.

THE RETAILER AS A BRAND

Think of some well-known retailers: Marks & Spencer, Boots, Sainsbury's, IKEA, The Body Shop, Next, Benetton. These are clearly all brands in the sense we have been using the word, some of them indeed international brands. They have a very strong identity in their customers' minds; when we go to one, we have a precise expectation of what we shall find, what level of quality and what value proposition. They have their core values, expressed in everything they do: their range and assortment of goods, the design and layout of their stores, the quality and training of their staff – in a phrase, *the total service they deliver*. As brands in their own right, they need the same discipline and commitment to maintenance and improvement as any other brand. The disaster that befell Ratner's after their chairman publicly described some of his goods as 'crap' is an awful reminder that the public's trust can easily be undermined.

As services, retailers have certain specific challenges in branding, and we shall return to those in the next chapter. For the moment, we will return to the issues posed to manufacturers.

THE ROLE OF OWN LABEL

Some of the retailers mentioned, notably Marks & Spencer, sell *only* their own label brand. Though fascinating in their own right, these retailers are not relevant to branded manufacturers except as customers for own label products. Whether or not to supply own label is certainly a question that most manufacturers should have considered, but it is not one we shall pursue in detail here – though it must form part of any treatment of the manufacturer–retailer relationship (for a fuller discussion see Randall, 1994).

The type of own label that concerns us here is that sold under the retailer's name as an alternative to manufacturers' brands. These own labels – or private labels, retailers' brands, distributors' own brands, and so on – are most prominent in supermarkets, but can also be found in many other fields. The part they play has changed from the days when they were just cheap, inferior imitations of a national brand – though some still are. It is vital that the manufacturer sees them objectively. The main points about own label are:

■ The quality is sometimes as good – in many categories, consumers perceive the quality of own labels as *at least as good* as the national brands; that is, they are not just a cheap substitute.
■ They have a strategic role in differentiating the retailer from competitors and building its identity.
■ They can form a brand in their own right either under the retailer's name or under a range or individual name.
■ They are also a price fighter, normally perceptibly cheaper than the leading brand.

The strategic role is key. Some retailers have made own label central to their strategy, Sainsbury's being the best-known example: around 65 per cent of their sales are their own brand. The other grocery majors have also been increasing their own label effort, and have between 47 and 55 per cent (Nielsen, *The British Shopper*, 1996).

As to category, there is a huge variation – from under 10 per cent own label to over 80 per cent. Not surprisingly, the categories with the lowest penetration are those with the strongest manufacturers' brands. The categories with low own label penetration, such as dentifrice (toothpaste to us), household cleaners, dog and cat food, or detergents, are characterized by extensive manufacturer activity, investment in technology and, in some cases (eg ethical pharmaceuticals), consumer reluctance to buy own label.

On the other hand, categories with high own label penetration usually show surplus manufacturing capacity, commodity status, low technical barriers, little product differentiation and low manufacturer investment. These underline the arguments made in this book: brands need investment and commitment; they will not survive on their own.

Perhaps surprisingly, *there is no correlation between own label penetration and level of price difference*. Strong brands can sustain sales even against severe price competition from own label – and sometimes this is very severe indeed. This is a real example of prices in a supermarket for the 'same' product:

▇ manufacturer's brand: 70p;
▇ retailer's own label: 20p;
▇ retailer's generic: 7p.

(A 'generic' is a very basic product offered in plain packaging in a limited range of commodity fields.)

As a corollary, the product categories containing strong brands showed much greater spending on advertising. For example, the advertising to sales ratio for the 10 categories with lowest own label share is 7.3, and for the 10 categories with highest own label share it is 1.4.

In grocery anyway, the categories seem to fall into four distinct types, classed by Simon Broadbent as follows:

▓ *Variety.* The top three brands plus own label account for less than 80 per cent of the market. These form half of all categories, are the largest, and account for 80 per cent of total turnover.

▓ *Top three.* The top three brands account for more than 75 per cent of the market, and own label averages 9 per cent. These form 15–20 per cent of all categories.

▓ *Head to head.* The top three brands take on average 60 per cent, the own label 30 per cent and others 10 per cent.

▓ *Own label.* The own label takes at least 40 per cent (on average 60 per cent), and the top three brands 30 per cent.

These differences have arisen over time, and must reflect fundamental product characteristics to some extent, but it is tempting to repeat that strong brands demand investment and support: where those are present, brands resist the attack of own label. If manufacturers are unable – for whatever reason – to deliver real, differentiated consumer benefits, then own label will take over.

'We will get rid of the brand tax consumers pay by cutting out the huge costs of marketing, so that retailers can make a good profit.' This is the public position taken by Cott Corporation, which has already shaken up some markets by producing acceptable substitutes for leading brands such as Coca-Cola. They claim to be working on 100 new retailer brands. The role of own label is likely to increase rather than decrease, especially in countries that are less developed than Britain. Only continuing investment in manufacturers' brands by their owners will stem the tide.

HOW THE RETAILER SEES MANUFACTURERS AND THEIR BRANDS

In dealing with this new situation of retailer power, in which retailers have more power than ever, manufacturers must apply basic marketing principles to their customers – retailers – as well as to consumers. The first step is to see brands as retailers see them.

How retailers see brands

Retailers see brands in a variety of ways. A *must stock* brand is a traffic builder, pulling people into the stores; there are no substitutes. A *known value item* (KVI) is bought frequently and is a staple item; the price of the leading brands is well known. A *brand leader* is the number one (and perhaps number two) brand in the category (if not covered above); it will probably be stocked as people will expect it. A *profit brand* is a brand that, whether through volume or margin or a combination of both, offers an attractive profit. More sophisticated retailers will calculate this on a 'DPP' basis (direct product profitability, ie taking into account *all* costs including storage and handling, and trying to optimize cube space).

A *variety* or *choice* or *niche brand* is one that provides variety by being different in some way (eg Baxter's soups). Finally, retailers *may* accept a *fighting brand*: a manufacturer's brand that positions itself as a value-for-money (ie cheap) brand, though from the supplier's point of view it is competing with the own label.

Manufacturers must be rigorous and objective in their approach to marketing their brands to retailers. Brands that do not meet any of these criteria will be de-listed.

De-listing is the ultimate threat wielded by retailers – and they do use it – so the manufacturer must be ready. One multiple retailer made demands that the supplier – a manufacturer of the leading brands in the category – refused to meet. All brands were de-listed. Six months later, the supplier was able to show research figures that demonstrated that, although the retailer's share of the total market was 10 per cent, its share of this category had fallen to only 6 per cent; they were losing sales and profits. The brands were re-listed.

How retailers see manufacturers

Retailers have a relationship not only with a brand, but also with a brand's manufacturer. They will be interested in how well you, the manufacturer, respond to a wide variety of their demands.

For example, what volumes and margins do your brands provide compared with the other brands in the category? How good is your customer service level – defined in *their* terms, not yours. How well are you meeting their expectations for delivery time, accuracy, invoicing error, etc? How good are the people dealing with the customer? Often the calibre of retailer staff is now very high, and your account managers may need further training.

How well do you cope with the unexpected, how far do you go to meet their demands – however difficult? What is your new product development record: usually well-planned and successful, a few mishaps, frequently shambolic? Do they prefer to deal with you rather than any of your competitors? And finally, how good are your brands, *really*?

THE WAY FORWARD – PARTNERSHIP?

This book is about branding, and there is not room for an extended discussion of trade marketing or dealing with retailers. However, it is obvious that today – and in the foreseeable future – retailers play a huge role in the actual delivery of the brand to consumers. Manufacturers must develop a twin focus on customers *and* consumers. They should see retailers as partners, and work *with* them to develop mutual benefits of greater sales and profits. Obviously there can never be total openness on either side, but trust and communication are preferable to their absence. The trend towards integrated supply chain management will encourage even closer working relationships.

The aim of the manufacturer must be to achieve preferred supplier status with its major customers, as long as that delivers satisfactory profits.

8

Branding in Service Businesses

Many people today argue that *all* businesses are service businesses. Even manufacturers provide services as well as physical products, and these service elements are becoming more and more important. Before- and after-sales service, reliable supply, timely delivery, responsiveness, development of EDI (electronic data interchange) systems or an extranet, and so on – all are services, and increasingly used to differentiate manufacturing firms from each other.

Equally, there are very few *pure* services. The physical constituents of the services provided by hotels, airlines, restaurants, retailers and many other services are central to our experience of them. A notable exception to this is financial services sold by telephone or on the Internet; they have almost no physical components – but they are unusual.

Most firms, then, are delivering a mixture of physical product and non-physical service. In this chapter we will concentrate on the service element, and on those businesses classified as services – but the lessons apply to all.

WHAT IS DIFFERENT ABOUT SERVICES?

Services *are* different from products in several ways that affect our approach to branding. First, they are *intangible*: we cannot see, feel or touch them. Whereas a Ford car, a Bang and Olufsen stereo or a Mars Bar are very much *there* and present to remind us of exactly what they are, a service is not. Second, services are *perishable*: a service cannot be stored like a product. An airline ticket or theatre seat not sold today is lost forever. Services are also *inseparable*: the service comes into existence only at the moment of delivery and consumption. Finally, services are *variable*: they are necessarily supplied by *people*, and people cannot be controlled precisely. Manufacturing processes can be managed so that all the products are virtually identical within given tolerances; the service delivered by one individual in one place at a certain time will vary from that given by someone else on a different occasion.

One implication of this is that marketing and operations functions in a service firm are – or ought to be – even more closely intertwined than in a manufacturing company. As Bob Townsend, the man who turned round the car rental firm Avis, famously said, 'Everyone in the company is the marketing department.'

To some extent, everyone *is* involved in some way in delivering the quality of service, though it is not always easy for them all to see this in a very large firm. Certainly it implies that internal marketing of the brand's core values to all employees must form part of the total brand-building effort. If staff are delivering the brand, they must know what it is they are expected to deliver.

PROBLEMS IN THE BRANDING OF SERVICES

No branding is without its problems – as we have seen – but services have some extra ones all to themselves.

Services can be copied

An idea cannot be patented, so services can be copied by competitors. Of course, in many markets physical products can also be copied in time, but a service can usually be reproduced more easily and quickly.

Services are difficult to encapsulate and communicate

The very intangibility of a service makes it extremely difficult to sum up. A physical product can be shown, displayed, seen and felt. The advertising can show pictures of it, and its presence in a store or in the home or workplace is a constant reminder of what it is. Encapsulating and expressing the essence of a service brand is a real challenge; the attempts of some firms to meet it sometimes smack of desperation.

Consumers are involved in production

Although buyers and users are not always actually present at the delivery of a service, they frequently are – and they are always involved in some way. There are two sorts of situation: one in which many consumers are present and one in which no other consumers are present. In a restaurant, theatre, hotel, or aeroplane, for example, other people are with us while we experience the service. This may be positive – watching a play in an empty theatre would be a less enjoyable experience than in a full one – but it also carries clear dangers (queuing, slow service, etc). From a branding point of view, the difficulty is that we need to make sure that all the other people are contributing to the desired brand, not detracting from it. Are they 'our sort of person'? Are they behaving in a way that reflects the brand values and enhances our experience of it?

If other consumers are not present, as with consultancy or professional advice, the problem is less complex. We still need to control our buyer/user in some way, but the issue is in principle no different from that of ensuring that people use our physical product in the way we wish them to – an important and often underestimated problem.

Quality is hard to evaluate and communicate

Services cannot be laid side by side and compared; we cannot carry out physical tests on them. Where standards such as ISO 9000 (the quality standard of the International Standards Organisation) and certifying bodies exist, we can certify that the service meets certain specifications but these are difficult to communicate to customers. Because services vary, it is hard to compare like with like, so it is especially difficult for buyers to judge value for money. This makes pricing a problem.

Standardization and quality control are difficult

One essential part of branding is the guarantee that the brand as delivered will always be what is expected. Given the variability of humans, this is impossible to control precisely. Indeed, whatever solutions we adopt (see below), there is a paradox built into service brands. An individual who is highly motivated and empowered will almost certainly give the best service; but the more we try to impose control and standardization, the less empowered that employee will be. This tension between empowerment and control seems inescapable.

No inventory is possible

Most services cannot be stored. If availability or responsiveness are part of the brand's core values, this may cause problems when demand fluctuates. Either extra staff must be employed to cope with peak demand – thereby raising costs – or some dissatisfaction will be caused.

POSSIBLE SOLUTIONS

The very existence of global service brands means that the problems are not insoluble. All airlines fly identical aircraft on the same routes between the same airports; they mainly charge very similar prices. Yet British Airways and Singapore Airlines – to name just two – have successfully developed true brands. How?

Exploit additional elements

Service businesses have some extra weapons that products lack. As well as offering the usual 'four Ps' of the normal marketing mix – product, price, promotion and place – services have three additional elements – people, process and physical evidence.

Clearly people are the central element to any service. Singapore Airlines, for example, decided to differentiate itself on service, and has communicated the quality of its service through its long-running 'Singapore girl' advertising campaign. Despite some controversy about whether this is sexist and demeaning to the women, there is no doubt that it has communicated the core values of attentiveness, charm and personal service extremely well. Staff selection and training ensure that the promise is actually delivered consistently.

Beyond that, Singapore Airlines are also using technology to try to improve the quality of the process. For business passengers, individual requirements can be captured and stored on a database so that preferences for drinks, meals, seating positions and so on can be delivered immediately. To be greeted by name with a smile, your favourite *brand* of your favourite drink, and the promise of your chosen meal when you want it – rather than when the airline finds it convenient – add up to superior service. They are developing the process to deliver a better service that is consistent with the brand's values.

At the other extreme, easyJet, the low-price airline, advertises itself with the slogan: 'If you want a meal, find a restaurant.' It is differentiating itself by offering not just a very cheap fare, but an explanation of why it is cheaper, and that this is not due to a compromise on safety.

As to physical evidence, this is clear with businesses such as fast food outlets, where the décor and cleanliness of the premises are part of the total offer. In other cases it may be more subtle: Abercrombie and Kent, who provide upmarket travel services, give their clients a leather ticket wallet and luggage label.

Innovate continuously

If each service development can be copied – and if they are seen to work, they quickly are copied – the only answer is to keep innovating to stay ahead. This is, in essence, the problem that very many brands – both products and services – face all the time. It comes back to the need to invest not only in the brand, but also in personnel; all personnel should be involved in thinking about possible improvements. The other essential is to have a truly customer-oriented view, looking for changes rather than resisting them.

Make the brand tangible

If it is difficult to encapsulate intangible attributes, then try to find a way of summarizing the brand in a tangible form. If the service is delivered through physical premises or objects, then this is fairly straightforward; normal design techniques can give the stores, bank premises and so on concrete characteristics that embody the brand's values. All The Body Shops have the same appearance and use identical colours; Crabtree and Evelyn stores carefully reflect the traditional English values the brand seeks to project – even though it is American and recently invented. McDonald's – the most famous example – has clearly recognizable outlets, summarized in the 'golden arches'.

What is more challenging is to find an emblem for the service itself. Singapore Airlines uses pictures of its hostesses to sum up its approach to hospitality, and this approach has stayed constant through many developments in the actual advertisements.

At a further remove, Lloyds Bank has adopted a black horse from its crest, and used it to communicate not only identity but certain values – sturdiness, perhaps even beauty and grace. It is not so far from the Jolly Green Giant, which symbolizes canned foods.

Use personal rather than impersonal sources

Many service firms, while using impersonal media such as television advertising, try to humanize the service. BT's advertisements – with Maureen Lipman's 'Beattie' character and subsequently Bob Hoskins reminding us that 'It's good to talk' – use this approach. This goes beyond mere product endorsement to trying to communicate, in a *personal* way, the benefits of the service.

An allied technique is to stimulate word-of-mouth – always the best form of recommendation and often using the methods suggested to achieve fame set out in Chapter 6.

Develop a continuing relationship

While this is an aim of all brands, it may be particularly relevant for services, as it gives a means of drawing attention to quality and reminding customers of the brand's values. The use of databases and direct marketing provides enormous potential for this approach.

It is vital that all communications be monitored to make sure that different sources are saying the same thing, and that the values being communicated are updated.

American Express found out that their direct mail literature and brochures were designed by different parts of the company, and looked as if they were from quite different firms. Worse, the tone developed by them during the 1980s was communicating values of prestige, exclusiveness and privilege – values felt to be out of tune with the 1990s. As Russ Shaw, then head of advertising and brand management of American Express in Europe, said:

> Our tone and manner should reflect those of a service company … a group which consistently reinvents itself to meet and exceed its customers' changing needs and expectations. Our voice should no longer be from the 'Chairman of the Club's membership's Committee' or from a disembodied global corporation that's full of itself. Rather it should be the voice of a consultant … a skilled, flexible and entrepreneurial advisor and supplier. Someone who earns his customer's trust through performance not promises. A competent, confident professional.
>
> (quoted in Macrae, 1996, p 56)

Notably, this method also uses the personalizing approach, and is used to communicate the continuous improvements that American Express tries to deliver.

Manage consumers

To avoid some of the problems of inseparability, consumers have to be managed. This is partly a matter of designing the process so that negatives do not arise, and partly of developing additions to mitigate the effects of negatives. For example, supermarkets led by Tesco now promise to put on extra checkout staff if more than two customers are waiting. At Disneyland Europe, entertainers keep waiting crowds amused as they queue for popular rides.

Industrialize the service

One way of ensuring standardization is to make the whole process identical in every outlet. McDonald's, the premier exponent of this approach, not only controls every ingredient, but has designed every aspect of the service delivery so that – as far as possible – it will always be the same.

While some argue that this will work only in certain categories such as fast food, the technique could be applied to parts of most service operations. Even in professional firms, which claim to deliver completely individual service, parts of the process are the same and can be standardized.

Select and train staff carefully

All service firms – wherever they are on the empowerment–control spectrum – need to recruit and train staff with the utmost care. The case of British Airways is well known: they spent millions on putting their many thousands of employees through intensive customer care programmes. Such programmes need to go beyond what is called the 'Have a nice day' syndrome to inculcate a real understanding of what the brand stands for and how the staff involved affect delivery.

Disney, probably the finest exponent of customer care in the world, has the most rigorous recruitment and selection programme, and trains its 'cast members' thoroughly. The Disney approach is very American, and many Europeans think it would not work elsewhere; but there is no reason it should not be adapted to local conditions, as in France. The basic premise is that the consumer's enjoyment is the only measure of success. *Everyone* contributes to that.

Logically, incentives and rewards should reflect the level of service delivered. Richer Sounds, a small UK retailer of hi-fi equipment, rewards staff on the basis of customer feedback measures, not on sales. It also uses imaginative rewards, including the use of the company Bentley for a month for the most successful branch. Virtually everything Richer Sounds does is geared to satisfying customers first. Sales and profits follow; and they do – Richer Sounds has the highest sales per square foot in the UK.

Obviously, the nature of the training must be geared to the brand concerned, and what suits one company will not necessarily suit another. If people are the key, however, then selection and training are central to the brand.

Manage demand

Sensible firms use flexible staffing to cope with fluctuations in demand, and most now at least try to match supply to the periods when most customers want to use the service – though it is only comparatively recently that banks, for example, learned this lesson.

Managing demand is more difficult, and most marketing people would love to know the secret. Unfortunately, there is no one secret, and the only answer is to use all available techniques – especially pricing – to even out peaks and troughs.

We can summarize by saying that many of the issues in branding services are identical to those in branding products. There are some additional difficulties, but leading service brands have shown the way. Commitment to service, listening to customers, internal marketing, staff training, and imaginative approaches to identity and communication form a basis which any service can profitably adopt.

9

Branding in Business-to-Business Markets

Brands exist in business-to-business markets. We have already mentioned IBM and Singapore Airlines, who are aiming their branding mainly at the profitable business market. In the computer market there are other brands such as Compaq and Microsoft, and sub-brands such as Windows, Word, WordPerfect, Lotus 1-2-3 and Quicken. There has even been the attempt to brand a component, in Intel's famous 'Intel Inside' campaign (to which we return later).

In the pharmaceutical field, many companies spend large sums branding their drugs even when they are under patent. One reason for this is to help them withstand the competition from generics when the patent runs out. Tagamet and Zantac are well-known names and still huge sellers; I still think of my asthma inhaler as Becotide, though my doctor tells me to ask for beclomethasone diproprionate.

Some companies use hierarchical branding structures just like their fmcg counterparts. ICI not only brands itself, but also its sub-brands. 3M had 1,500 brand names spread over its 60,000 products; it has now rationalized them into three categories: 1) 3M plus generic product description; 2) 3M plus sub-brand plus description (eg 3M Scotchmate hook and loop); and 3) new brand name (allowed very rarely).

On the other hand, branding is relatively underdeveloped

compared with consumer markets. Many in the field doubt its value, seeing it merely as unnecessary froth. Certainly, some very bad attempts at branding have achieved nothing. Just adding a 'clever' name to a basic commodity product – as was tried in the United States with plywood – will not create a brand. Indeed, it will probably do little except add extra costs without increasing sales.

As with services, let us first look at what is actually different about business-to-business markets, and then see how branding can be applied.

DIFFERENCES IN BUSINESS-TO-BUSINESS MARKETS

There are of course overlaps between consumer and business-to-business (or 'industrial' or 'organizational') markets. Both firms and individuals buy cars, stationery, and cleaning materials, for example. Business markets cover a huge range, and generalization is dangerous – but there are some basic differences.

Rationality

It is often said that business buying decisions are rational compared with those made by consumers. We may stress that most consumers are also fairly rational – after all, they include the same people who make the business decisions. It is true that in many business purchases, there is a detailed structure of evaluation based on objective measurements, and that is rarely found among consumers. On the other hand, we must always remember that managers are also ordinary people, and they have human motivations at work. Buyers' feelings can affect their decisions, in two ways: 1) their *career* is important, and they may feel that they do not want to make a mistake, or they want to look good in the eyes of a superior; and 2) they also have *personal* feelings such as friendship, loyalty and trust.

Buyer–seller relationship

In contrast to fmcg manufacturers – who are now just beginning to realize that they need to develop a relationship with their consumers – the business market has known for many years that the long-term relationship is the foundation of its operations. This has become more and more important as many firms have cut down the number of suppliers and try to work with a smaller number of them as partners. This is happening across many sectors; it is driven partly by such techniques as just-in-time delivery, EDI (Electronic Data Interchange) and the Internet, and also by the belief that the new, open and co-operative relationship is more productive than the old adversarial one.

Many of these relationships are very close, and new products, for example, are developed through detailed co-operation.

Complexity

Business buying decisions are more complex than those made by consumers. Leaving aside the paper-clip type of purchase, most business buying decisions are about situations considerably more complicated than those found in consumers' lives. Similarly, the purchase is usually fairly technical, involving expertise on both sides.

Number of people involved

There are also more people involved in business buying decisions. Individual consumer purchases involve only a few people. In organizational buying, however, there may be many more – up to 20 or so. These people will be in different parts of the organization; they will have different criteria for making the purchasing decision and therefore will exert their influence at different times in the purchase cycle.

In a typically complex decision, people from engineering, manufacturing, maintenance, finance and purchasing may be involved at different times. They will have different objectives and criteria, and cannot all be reached by the same message or the same method.

Decision time

Because of the complexity of the decision – and the number of people involved – the process may take several months, or even years for very large purchases.

Impact of purchase

The impact of a purchase can be far greater for business markets than for the consumer. Something bought by a company may be absolutely crucial to its future. If it is a vital part of the process – a machine tool, a major component, a computer system – the very survival of the firm may depend on it.

Importance of service, delivery and reliability

Because a purchase can be crucial to the future of a company, service, delivery and reliability have a major importance in business markets. While we should not underestimate the importance of these in consumer markets, they are likely to weigh much more heavily in business purchases. Again, the ability of the firm to carry out its business may depend on reliable supplies of materials or components. Price may then become a secondary consideration.

Total cost

Finally, business markets view the cost of a purchase in a different way than individual consumers. Consumers normally look just at the initial purchase price, but businesses examine the total cost of the item over its useful life. Thus Mercedes advertises to finance directors, reminding them that while the initial price of a Mercedes as a company car may look high, its resale value means that its total cost will be much more competitive. With more complex equipment, the price calculation becomes even more influential.

HOW ORGANIZATIONS BUY

We have seen that several people are involved in buying decisions. They are known collectively as the *decision-making unit* or 'DMU'. One of the key tasks in marketing to businesses is to identify the members of this DMU, and to understand how to reach and influence them.

The DMU members play several roles – in a small firm, one person may play many or even all roles, while in a large organization there may be more than one person in each role. The roles are:

■ *User.* The person who actually uses the product or service; he or she will clearly have specific requirements and views.

■ *Influencer.* An influencer may be in an official position (eg an IT adviser) or may be someone inside or even outside the firm whose views carry weight. Many suspect that influencers are often found in golf clubs, sports changing rooms or membership organizations.

■ *Gatekeeper.* A gatekeeper is someone who controls the flow of information to the other members of the DMU. It may be the purchasing manager, but it could also be the chief executive's secretary. Knowing who the members of the DMU are is the starting point to ensuring that each of them gets the information he or she needs.

■ *Decider.* Often there is one individual who makes the final decision. This is most likely to be the most senior member – say the chief executive in a very important purchase – but could be another member of the team. It may be a different person for different occasions within the same organization, and may vary from firm to firm as to formal position.

■ *Buyer.* Most purchases have to be signed off, frequently by the designated purchasing manager; but it may be a different manager, say the production director or head of finance.

Finding out who exactly performs each role – and keeping that information up to date over time – is a subtle and sensitive task, but essential to success.

One approach that may help is shown in Figure 9.1. While a purchasing manager alone may make decisions on low-value items, more and more people will become involved as:

1. the buying firm becomes larger;
2. the firm has little experience of buying or using the brand;
3. there is weak loyalty towards the supplier;
4. the brand is more important in the buyer's production process;
5. the financial size of the order increases; and
6. individuals perceive risk of any kind in buying the brand (de Chernatony and McDonald, 1992, p 108).

It helps to classify the purchase as straight re-buy, modified re-buy or new buy. The newer or more unfamiliar the purchase, the more

		Low	High
Product	High	User with specialist knowledge dominant	Company-wide involvement
or			
service			Purchasing manager and financial advisers dominant
complexity	Low	Purchasing manager dominant	
		Low	High

Commercial risk

Source: de Chernatony and McDonald, 1992, p 108

Figure 9.1 *Predicting who will be involved in purchasing*

– and more senior – people will become involved. It is worth bearing in mind that normally a brand name is most trusted when buyers are unfamiliar with the field, or see high risk.

The type of purchase will highlight the varying importance of buying criteria. For example, for straight re-buy situations, reliability and price will be most important; in newer situations, factors such as technical service and quality of training offered will loom larger. Again, reputation will be most important in situations of greatest uncertainty.

It is also useful to know what stage in the buying process has been reached. The standard model of the stages (see Robinson, Faris and Wind, 1967) is:

1. anticipation or recognition of a problem;
2. determination of what purchase is needed;
3. specification of the characteristics and quantity required;
4. search and qualification of potential suppliers;
5. acquisition of proposals;
6. evaluation of proposals and selection of supplier;
7. selection of order routine; and
8. performance feedback and evaluation.

The earlier in the process a supplier can contribute, the greater the chance of success. Often, the main problem is 'getting on the list', and it is here that branding may help: buyers will be readier to accept a name they know, even if they are not currently customers.

Another aspect of business markets is that the product may be sold into quite different types of organization, and they may have different criteria for making purchases.

DEVELOPING A BUSINESS BRAND

As with fmcg brands, the performance of the product will be the foundation of what ultimately drives the establishment of a business brand. As we have seen, performance and reliability are even more crucial to businesses, and it must never be forgotten that no amount of additional marketing effort can compensate for poor performance. IBM's computers may not have been technologically innovative, but they have always been high-quality machines that worked well.

At a fundamental level, marketing and branding depend on a deep understanding of the customer's needs. The product must be seen from the customer's point of view; as the chairman of Carborundum said, 'Our customers don't want grinding wheels, they want metal removed.' This may imply offering a package of products and services that together meet the customer's needs; your own product may be the centrepiece, but may be complemented by other items bought in. This is the concept of the 'augmented product', which can differentiate the supplier who is really in tune with the customer's situation.

Other elements of the product that are vital in consumer brands are the name and packaging. *Design* is important in business markets too – though often neglected, particularly in Britain. Design in this sense goes beyond the technical, functional input that is obviously fundamental. It should also include branding: how does the *look* of the product sum up and transmit brand values? Some products may need to look chunky and tough; others may need to suggest that they are the latest thing, at the leading edge.

In one experiment, two models of the same piece of instrumentation equipment were evaluated by technical people. One model was plain and the other was styled, with some colour added. The 'prettier' model was rated higher – not only for appearance, but on technical aspects too. Even engineers are susceptible to beauty.

The role of advertising

The big difference between business markets and fmcg brands comes with the role of advertising. Though the product itself is fundamental, consumer brands are established and supported mainly by heavy advertising, as we have seen. In business markets, on the contrary, advertising plays a much smaller role. Few business-to-business firms spend as much as one per cent of sales on advertising. Because of the nature of the relationship and the buying process, *personal selling* is the main communication tool. The quality, training and deployment of the sales force then become paramount. Other people will have contact with customers, but the sales person will always be the main contact.

The sales people still need support, however, and this is where advertising comes in. Advertising can introduce the firm and its products, laying the foundation for a personal visit. A sales person calling cold, from a firm the buyer has not even heard of, will probably not even get a hearing. A selling campaign *backed by advertising* will have greater impact – and produce higher sales – than personal selling alone.

The advertising should take the same role as in consumer markets – of transmitting brand values. Major companies even use television advertising to develop their brands: the airlines, ICI and IBM spring to mind. If the firm's customers are numerous enough, and spread over a wide range of industries and organizational functions, then TV advertising can make sense. It has greater impact – and is better at building brands – than any other medium.

Most companies cannot afford that sort of expenditure. They use trade magazines and specialist publications. The key is to base the campaign on the analysis of the DMU described above. Which people are we trying to reach, and what message are we trying to put over to them? The message from Mercedes to finance directors mentioned above appeared in *The Economist*; similar messages appear in the *Financial Times*. Other advertisements aimed at production directors and purchasing managers appear in the specialist publications that they normally read.

A glance through some of these will suggest that there are some companies who have worked out exactly what they are trying to do, and who use professional advertising to communicate relevant messages. There are, unfortunately, too many others who seem to have no clear idea what the advertising is supposed to be doing; they are merely going through the motions. It is not surprising that the target audience can be dismissive of advertising in general, seeing what they are exposed to. Well-targeted advertising as part of a complete marketing campaign can and does produce results.

Trade fairs and exhibitions

As part of the personal selling effort, trade fairs and exhibitions are prime methods of contact and communication in business markets. The points made above about the quality of people rule here too. The design aspect is again central, as this may be the most visible face of your firm to many potential customers. Design should be part of the branding process, and should cover every aspect of the firm's physical appearance. Everything should be co-ordinated, and be sending consistent messages. (The issue of corporate identity will be discussed in the next chapter.) Public appearances are opportunities to remind customers of the brand identity and reinforce brand values.

Other promotion

If advertising is suspect to many hard-headed business people, then promotion is even more so. It smacks of plastic daffodils, coupons and tacky competitions. As with fmcg brands, however, there is a right and a wrong way to use promotion. Although it plays little part in most industrial marketing campaigns, when it is used well it can be very effective.

A good example is the dancing excavator show mounted by J C Bamford (manufacturer of excavators, back-hoes and similar machines). The company has shrewdly built up its brand to the extent that JCB is now almost a generic term for small earth-moving equipment. This has been done not just through promotion, but through the consistent quality of the product, a good sales force, excellent distribution and advertising. The dancing excavator extravaganza, in which a line of machines performs a dance routine at trade shows, just adds a note of excitement in what might otherwise be a rather dull world. It is also excellent publicity – and worth many column inches in the press! It is, let us note, quite consistent with the brand's values, and incidentally a good demonstration of the product's qualities.

Any other form of promotion, including sponsorship, should be judged by the same criteria: what is the audience, what is the message, how does it enhance brand values? Carefully selected sponsorship can fulfil many useful purposes, including giving opportunities to develop relationships with a range of people from customer firms, and indeed with your own staff from different departments and locations.

WHEN IS IT WORTH DEVELOPING A BUSINESS BRAND?

There are, then, many successful business brands in a variety of industries. Do they have anything in common, and are there any rules to guide aspiring brand builders?

The first question is whether the company or individual products should be the brand. (The issue of the company as brand is so important that the next chapter is devoted to it.) Obviously, it is particularly pertinent for business-to-business marketers, but we shall postpone comment for now.

As to whether to develop a brand at all, it should be clear that it takes *commitment, time and money*. A half-hearted attempt is worse than not trying. It will alienate some customers, and dishearten many staff.

The decision to develop a brand must be taken at board level, with a full knowledge of the resources available and an objective view of the company's strengths and weaknesses. Unfortunately, putting a value on the benefits to be expected from a successful attempt is impossible. This might put some boards off, but then again they make other major commitments without reliable information about payoffs – think of investments in IT systems, or training.

There are no rules, but let us examine some of the reasons firms have made the commitment.

Competitors are doing it

Competitive action is a powerful motivator. Many airlines have followed British Airways and Singapore Airlines in trying to develop their brand. Few have shown the same level of understanding of what is involved – or the commitment to see it through. The question to ask is, 'What benefits are the competitors getting out of the brand?' If they are achieving higher growth rates, greater customer loyalty or better success rates with new products, is that due to the brand or to other factors? The establishment of a very strong brand did not make IBM unassailable – though it may have contributed to its survival and recovery.

Support many new products

The approach of 3M shows how a company can use the power of a brand – when it is properly structured and co-ordinated – to help launch a range of new products in a variety of markets. 3M is probably the most innovative large company in the world. It knows that it is going to go on launching scores, even hundreds, of new products every year. Now that it has built a clear brand architecture, it can use the increasing strength of the brand; if I have bought and been happy with 3M Scotch tape, Post-It notes and computer diskettes, I shall be ready to try its new adhesive.

Build demand for components

In a famous example, Intel has been building the brand of its chips – even though most purchasers never see one. It is a useful illustration in that it has been very successful in raising awareness of, and apparently demand for, its Pentium chip. On the other hand, Intel probably received a lot more publicity and criticism when a tiny flaw was discovered in its operation than it would have done without the brand building.

Supporting spare parts

In many industries, the sale of spare parts forms a major share of total revenue – and is often more profitable than selling the original equipment. Imitation spare parts sold at a much cheaper price pose a threat to this business, and additionally may damage the reputation of the main brand because they are of inferior quality. Caterpillar, as an example, advertised to its customers reminding them of these risks and urging them to buy the genuine spares. It had, of course, spent many years building up the Caterpillar brand.

Going global

Firms that are already operating globally, or are approaching that point, may see advantages in a common brand, such as flexibility of supply, and economies of scale and scope. This is another important topic, which is discussed in Chapter 11.

Motivating staff and other audiences

Firms are competing in the markets not only for products but also for staff and for finance. A well-known brand can be an advantage in these, too. Good staff will be more attracted to a firm they know and which has a good reputation than to an obscure one. Existing staff will feel more involved and motivated – all other things being equal – if they are contributing to a famous brand. Investors are probably more attracted to famous firms – again all things being equal.

To sum up, brands can be built in business-to-business markets, and there are many successful examples. Any firms thinking of following them need to analyse carefully why they are doing so, and whether they have the top-level commitment and the resources needed. If they do decide to brand, they should apply the basic principles of marketing and branding, suitably adapted to their particular market.

10

The Company and the Brand

The brands discussed throughout this book show that many are *company brands* – that is, the name of the company identifies the brand. It was striking that when *The Economist* surveyed people in Japan, the United States and Europe, asking about familiarity with and esteem for brands, the list of *world brands* was:

1. Coca-Cola;
2. IBM;
3. Sony;
4. Porsche;
5. McDonald's;
6. Disney;
7. Honda;
8. Toyota;
9. Seiko;
10. BMW;
11. Volkswagen;
12. Mercedes Benz.

All are company brands, and they are evenly spread between Japan, Germany and the United States; not one brand from any other country appears on the list.

A slightly different exercise produced another list of great brands called the 'Interbrand Superleague':

1. Coca-Cola;
2. Kellogg's;
3. McDonald's;
4. Kodak;
5. Marlboro;
6. IBM;
7. American Express;
8. Sony;
9. Mercedes Benz;
10. Nescafé.

While there is some overlap, Interbrand's list introduces some individual brands: Marlboro and Nescafé. Their selection was based on their own expert opinion, using the criteria of:

▓ leadership;
▓ stability;
▓ market size;
▓ internationality;
▓ trend;
▓ support; and
▓ protection.

Is the preponderance of company brands an accident? Many would argue that it is not, and during the 1990s there have been many voices urging that the company brand is the future. Yet world-class branders such as Procter and Gamble, Mars and Unilever insist on individual brands – can they be wrong?

This chapter will summarize the arguments, and try to find a way through the thickets.

ARGUMENTS FOR THE COMPANY AS BRAND

In 1990, Stephen King wrote:

The company brand will become the main discriminator. That is, consumers' choice of what they buy will depend less upon an evaluation of the functional benefits to them of a product or service, rather more on their assessment of the people in the company behind it, their skills, attitudes, behaviour, design, style, language, greenism, altruism, modes of communication, speed of response, and so on – the whole company culture, in fact. In essence, brand building in the 1990s will ... be a lot closer to the marketing of services than to the brand building of the classic brands.

Later, Hamel and Prahalad, the most influential writers on strategy in the 1990s, added another argument. They argued that it now takes in the order of US $1 billion of advertising to build a significant share of mind with consumers across North America, Asia and Europe. 'Yet what is the marginal cost for Sony, in terms of brand building, when it launches a new product bearing those four famous letters?' they ask. 'The answer, of course, is that Sony's new product introductions benefit from instant street credibility... What Sony and other global brand leaders have done is consciously to build "banner brands" that span multiple products and businesses and which help customers transfer great experiences with today's products into great interest and enthusiasm for tomorrow's products... We believe that any company that fails to take advantage of the logic of banner branding will find itself, long-term, at a competitive disadvantage' (Hamel and Prahalad, 1994).

A similar argument was put in a BBC video on branding:

Until a few years ago, particularly if you were an fmcg company, the way to develop markets was within country and within product category. So you had a different brand in each country and product category and that was the level at which brands were operated. But now ... most brands have become so fragmented that they really do not have any share of voice in the global public's minds; so the result is that having hundreds and hundreds of separate brand channels actually puts the company at a disadvantage.

The real key is the legacy and history of how brands have been managed in the 1970s and 1980s. Many companies are now saddled in the 1990s with huge portfolios of small minority brands that do not justify themselves and are not supportable economically in the current communications environment, nor on any future competitive scenarios. (BBC video *Branding – the Marketing Advantage*, quoted in Macrae, 1996, p 158.)

Essentially, there are three arguments here in favour of the company as brand. The first is that consumers want a relationship with a company, and the reassurance that a trustworthy organization stands behind any brand they buy. It is certainly true that many companies want to develop the relationship with their customers, as we have seen. It is also true that in Japan consumers expect a large firm to stand behind its brands – but the situation in Japan is quite different from elsewhere and there is little evidence that we are going to follow them, either culturally or in industry structure. Some pressure groups seem anxious to identify the parent company, but only so that they can organize boycotts of all the brands of firms that offend them. Beyond that, it has to be said that there is little evidence that the mass of consumers are actively seeking relationships with the companies that provide the hundreds of products they buy – even if it were feasible.

The second argument is that all companies are service companies and must organize themselves as such. This is a more powerful argument, already discussed and accepted in this book. Making all departments in the firm recognize that they contribute to the delivery of the total service expected by customers and consumers will entail, logically, presenting the *company's* face – not just that of scores of individual brands.

Finally, it is no longer economically possible to sustain individual brands. This argument is more complex, and is bound up with the issue of internationalization (which will be covered in the next chapter). Clearly, there are economies of scale for companies such as Sony, but it is not clear that these would be automatically available to all firms, as we shall see below. It is true that, as we saw in Chapter 5, both Procter and Gamble, and Unilever have decided to reduce their brand portfolios substantially; it is no longer a feasible strategy to proliferate brands endlessly – but that is an argument against brand proliferation, not in favour of the company as brand.

ARGUMENTS AGAINST THE COMPANY AS BRAND

Counter-arguments to the trend towards the company brand are often based on the pragmatic view that, starting from where we are now, it is simply too difficult. The huge, global firms that we can take as representing the individual brand position – Procter and

Gamble, and Unilever, for instance – have so far set their face against reversing decades of history. The objections fall under several heads.

Too wide a range of products

The largest global corporations have hundreds or even thousands of products. In some (see Chapter 5) the range of markets is very wide indeed: General Electric of the United States operates in markets from consumer durables through electronics to heavy engineering and financial services. It is not clear that one over-arching brand essence could be found to cover this span. In Japan, admittedly, companies like Yamaha or Mitsubishi seem quite able to provide parentage to a surprisingly disparate brood – but this sort of stretch is rarely found elsewhere.

Risk of damaging heritage

Many individual brands have histories going back decades. Millions have been spent in building the brand, its identity and personality. The owners are rightly reluctant to do anything that risks disturbing this precious heritage, and introducing a hitherto unknown parent might do just that.

Too complicated to understand

Even if it were attempted, the resulting framework could be hugely complicated, and would just confuse consumers rather than comfort them. What would they make of a brand parentage that went through Persil to Lever Brothers to Unilever in Britain (but through different lineage in other countries), and showed cousins in quite different markets, sometimes with different names?

No clear benefit

If – as we must assume – most consumers are ignorant of the identity of the parent company but are very happy with the brand, what benefit would accrue to either? While people in the business community are familiar with Procter and Gamble, and Unilever, most consumers are not. What benefit would Marlboro buyers gain by knowing that it was owned by Philip Morris? Given the complex structures resulting from takeovers and mergers, ultimate parentage is often remote. Given also the instability of many corporations, it would be a pity – to say the least – to spend millions identifying a parent, only to find that the company has been sold or de-merged and now has a different parent. Think of the Nabisco subsidiaries in Europe, for example, which were all sold off after the KKR buyout.

Vulnerability to disaster

Disaster sometimes strikes a brand, whether as a result of human error, bad luck or sabotage. Perrier suffered from contamination by benzene, Tylenol from malicious sabotage and Ratner's from a foolish off-the-cuff remark by its chairman. Both Perrier and Tylenol were withdrawn from the shelves immediately; although they suffered temporary loss of share, they both recovered. Ratner's (a retailer of low-priced jewellery, and hitherto very successful) was very badly hit by Gerald Ratner's 'light-hearted' comment that its products were cheap because they were – in his singularly ill-chosen word – 'crap'. Ratner himself lost his job and the company's sales plummeted – it even had to change its name before it could start on the slow and painful road back to health.

Critics of the company as brand see this as a dreadful warning against the dangers of putting all your eggs in one basket: where a multi-brand owner might survive the death of one of its brands, the single-company brand might not.

So far, then, it seems that in some cases there may be benefits from branding the company, but in others there would also be serious problems. As the 3M example showed, some rationalization may be both possible and beneficial.

BRAND ARCHITECTURE

Even if a company is quite happy with its current position of having many individual brands, it must make sense at least to consider the alternatives. The case for rationalization depends on three conditions being met.

First, the *economic argument* must be true: it really will become impossible for a company to fund the development of its separate brands globally. Each firm will need to take its own view on this, as it is not yet proven.

Second, consumers must be able to perceive *genuine benefit* from linkages between a company's brand and other names. To put it at its most neutral, if the company wants to introduce a new branding level – pillar, umbrella or company – for motives such as saving money on packaging, then there must at least be no *disbenefit* to consumers.

Finally, the new structure should provide *new opportunities* for the company in creating new brands or markets, and should not limit freedom.

Let us agree that, as we said at the beginning of the book, the whole firm must be committed to its brands. Given the many challenges described in Chapter 3, every resource must be tapped and focused to build and maintain the brands, and some rationalization may help here. The phrase coined to describe the attempt to develop a new, rational structure in a multi-brand firm is 'brand architecture' (see for example Macrae, 1996).

What brand architecture tries to do is articulate the linkages and relationships between brands, so as to optimize the firm's efforts. We have seen that 3M has introduced new discipline into its brand structure so that all brands can gain from the quality reputation of the parent – in the way that all Sony products already do. Others are also starting to build more structure, though the discussion is muddied by the confusion between the terms employed: as we saw in Chapter 1, words like 'banner', 'umbrella' and 'pillar' are used in different senses by different people.

Let us assume that the terms refer to different levels in the branding structure. Some pillar or umbrella brands are familiar:

Umbrella/company	Pillar	Individual product
L'Oréal	Laboratoires Garnier	Hair care
Birds Eye	Steakhouse	Meat meals

What brand architecture can do is to clarify linkages so that brands in a genuine family can gain from their association. Heavy, brand-building advertising can work either at the umbrella and pillar levels – benefiting all the sub-brands – or at the sub-brand level but always mentioning the pillar – thus building that for the future.

Either way, the cumulative effect should be greater than totally separate brand spending.

For example, Unilever is using the 'Elida Institute' as an umbrella for hair care brands and the 'Pond Institute' for skin care. 'From the Elida Institute', like 'from Laboratoires Garnier', is a tag line in each brand advertisement that will gradually establish the pillar brand and its values – which can then be spread to other new sub-brands as they are launched.

The other gain from such an exercise is clarifying the exact function and objective of each brand. Some, for example, may be destined to be global brands, others regional or local. Some will be aimed at the number one or two spot, some at niches, some perhaps as fighting brands – low cost, low price, positioned against the own label. Such clarity will help reduce unnecessary and wasteful overlap, and should sharpen the focus of each brand.

This makes sense, but the next step is much less clear. Can the ultimate parent, Unilever, be brought into the structure? It is not immediately apparent that consumers would gain anything from this. For some companies, the final parent may be one branding stage too far. A situation in which an international brand, such as Magnum ice cream, appears in different countries under the name of different parents may be untidy – but it may also work. Radicals would argue that this is today's wisdom, and that in 10 or 20 years' time this untidiness will be a fatal flaw.

So, as usual, there are no absolute answers. There are possible gains from rationalization and clarification, and there are moves anyway to limit brand proliferation. For some firms, making the company the brand – at least as the parent and guarantor – will make sense. If the gains seem large enough, it is worth the upheaval and investment to move from a set of individual, unconnected brands to a clear structure headed by a caring, competent parent. It may take many years, but it seems the path down which many companies will be heading.

11

International and Global Brands

It is commonplace knowledge that the world is becoming more international. We talk of the 'global village', and follow events in countries we had not even heard of a few years ago. People now in middle age have a very different experience of the world from their parents, most of whom had never been abroad – except forcibly during a war. We travel, holiday abroad, eat foods from all over the world, and use products manufactured thousands of miles away. Our children have moved on even further, and view trips to Asia, Australia or South America at the age of 18 as normal.

This reflects and is reflected by changes in the business world, which has never been more open. Few markets are free from foreign competition, and most are seeing that competition grow each year. The famous brands we listed are international or global, and many brands aspire to that position. The debate about global brands and standardization has generated considerable heat, if not always much light. In this chapter we will look at the arguments for and against global branding and describe the conditions for success.

First, it is worth stating the obvious: that any company wanting to develop international or global brands should have a clear idea of why and what exactly are they trying to achieve. Profit, presumably – but is this the best way of increasing profit? Sometimes, as we shall see, internationalization is forced on a firm, but usually it is a choice. The firm needs to make sure that developing international or global brands is a coherent part of a total business strategy.

WHAT IS A GLOBAL BRAND?

The fact that there are indeed some global brands should not blind us to the fact that there are not all that many. Coca-Cola and McDonald's are famous examples of brands that appear to be the same the world over, and that have achieved remarkably wide distribution. Even they, however, vary their product to allow for local tastes. The variations are not great – slight changes in sweetness level for Coke, and local additions to the menu for McDonald's – but they exist. It is also true that a brand may appear similar, but in fact be *positioned* quite differently in the various countries in which it sells. (We shall return to this idea later.)

The Japanese car and consumer electronic manufacturers are as near as you can get to global brands, and the best of them have penetrated most of the 200 or so countries in the world – even they have to adapt to local laws, languages and structures.

However, many brands that we think of as global – because we see them in the airports and hotels we visit – have in fact very shallow penetration of many markets, and sell most of their volume in a few countries.

So the idea of a global brand as one that is *identical* in every respect in every country is a myth. Instead, a global brand can be loosely defined as one that:

■ is basically the same product or service everywhere, with only minor variations (Coca-Cola, Guinness);
■ has the same brand essence, identity and values (McDonald's, Sony);
■ uses the same strategic principles and positioning (Gillette); and
■ employs the same marketing mix as far as possible (Avon Cosmetics).

This definition, especially the last item, is not hard and fast. There is a grey area between global and international brands, but this hardly matters; in the real world, definitions are unimportant compared with strategic intent and detailed implementation. What matters is what the firm is trying to do, and how well it does it.

We must return, too, to the point that a brand's positioning may vary. McDonald's, for example, seems to be essentially the same brand the world over – the same name, appearance, basic promise and, with adaptation, products. Yet the consumer's perception of a visit to a McDonald's in the United States is quite different from that in Moscow or Thailand. To an American, McDonald's is everyday, low-priced, convenient, only one of many similar offerings. To those in developing countries, however, it is a treat – even a status symbol (Bullmore, 1999).

Budweiser is a mass-market, blue-collar beer in its home market in the United States, but in Britain it is positioned as a premium, foreign import. Does this matter? It does only if the target consumers are likely to be exposed to the differing positions and thereby confused. For most products, this will not happen. An American visiting Thailand will recognize the familiar McDonald's, and coming to Britain may be upset only by the price of a Bud.

The only markets in which confusion could arise are those in which a significant proportion of the target consumers travel frequently and widely. Thus hotels like Marriott that cater for business travellers will aim to be positioned in the same way everywhere, as will luxury brands like Chanel or Dunhill. The growth of international media such as satellite TV and the Internet offers arenas for possible confusion, and positions may need to be rationalized within their footprint.

INTERNATIONAL BRANDS

On the other side of the fuzzy line, brands that are sold in many countries but are not global are known as 'international' brands. These range from those that are standardized across a region to those that are different in every market in which they compete. The argument for such local adaptation is that local conditions make it essential; we shall return to this below.

ARGUMENTS FOR GLOBALIZATION

Commentators and business people have been arguing for years about globalization. The balance sways back and forth, and no single answer will emerge. The only possible answer to the questions, 'Should I make my brand global?' and 'Is it possible?' is 'It depends' – on the product, markets, consumers, competitors, politics and so on. Every product and market situation must be analysed afresh.

The main arguments in favour of globalization centre on the view that the world is not only getting smaller psychologically, but that it is also getting more similar.

Markets are becoming the same

People are basically the same and are becoming even more like each other all the time, says this argument. A world culture is developing, formed by global communications, travel, films, television and the activities of multinational firms. In the three areas that make up the so-called 'triad' – the United States, Europe and South Asia – this is arguably true *to an extent*. It is most true of younger people, and in many markets the tastes of the under-30s are probably very similar at least in most developed countries. It is a culture dominated by America – especially through films, TV and popular music – though other nations' products are accepted as the international standard: consider Japanese consumer electronics and French haute couture and allied perfumes. In business markets, America dominates most computer and software markets, but the standards are worldwide. Similarly, Japanese automation and earth-moving equipment and German engineering in many fields are world leaders, but the markets are essentially the same everywhere.

There is a segment in every market that is the same

All markets are very clearly *not* identical, because there are huge variations in economic development, wealth and culture. It is idle to argue that, even within a region, all countries are the same. Thailand is not the same as Japan, and Uruguay is not the same as Canada. Nevertheless, argue some, there will be a *segment* within each market that will be essentially similar to the segment found everywhere else. Thus there will be a segment that responds to Rolex, Dunhill and Gucci in every country, for example. The size of the segment will vary considerably, but it will exist. The extent to which this is true of markets outside the obvious luxury products is unclear but it certainly could be: there will be a segment that wants a particular type of car or toothpaste, in every country, but the size will vary.

Global economies of scale give unanswerable competitive advantage

Global scale offers, potentially at least, huge economies. The cost advantage this confers can be used either to offer unbeatable value or to invest in product development or promotion. Either way, local competitors will be unable to respond.

There are some markets that *need* global scale. It is hard for local firms to compete in civil aircraft, cars, or pharmaceuticals. Beyond that, the argument is more speculative. Theodore Levitt, one of the fiercest proponents of global branding, argued that economies of scale could actually overcome local market preferences. If a manufacturer ignored current differences in consumer preferences and offered a common product at an unbeatable price, consumers would trade off ideal preferences for value. For example, there have traditionally been differences in what European countries demand in a washing machine: some want automatic, others do not, some prefer front-loading and others top-loading, and so on. Levitt argued that making a single, standardized model on a European scale would offer such value for money that consumers would abandon their traditional views and buy it anyway. How far this argument applies in each market can be tested only in practice – and probably by actually trying it, not by market research.

That economies of scale can be found is probable. Unilever found that they were using 15 different cornets for one of their ice creams in Europe alone, and another part of the organization discovered that there were 16 different containers for Jif (called Cif in some countries) in the same region. Even service firms can usually find some economies, particularly in back-office processing – but every few hundred thousand pounds off costs are useful.

There are also possible savings in marketing costs such as advertising. What the marketing people must do is ensure that cost savings – in whatever area – do not damage the brand.

There is only one right idea

A more conceptual view is that, for any one brand at any particular time, there is only one correct strategy. The definition of the brand essence and identity, the target segment, the positioning, the principles of the mix and targeting have one best solution. Once that is found, it should be applied in every country with changes only where they are absolutely unavoidable – because of legislation, for instance.

This is not a belief in a Platonic ideal of a brand strategy: that it exists eternally, waiting for someone to find it. It is rather a view based on the experience that the top-flight talent needed to produce a winning brand strategy is thinly spread across the company. The company will not have such top people in every country, so local adaptations are likely to be less than optimal.

In one case, the chief executive of a multinational cosmetics company allowed local adaptations, and the firm made no profit. When he was ordered to start producing profits, he imposed standardization – based on the argument above – and the profits started to flow.

There is no doubt that many companies are developing global brands; the trend is in that direction. Not everyone agrees, however, and there are arguments for local marketing, too.

ARGUMENTS AGAINST GLOBALIZATION

Those who oppose global branding base their arguments on fundamental marketing principles: it is the job of marketing people to be sensitive to their customers and consumers, and only they – in the local country – really understand them.

Markets are actually different

It is easy to show that, even within a region such as Western Europe, there are significant differences between countries. The car market shows different preferences, and even if some of this is due to past government action, it is an additional argument for treating each local market as unique. Pasta is seen as old-fashioned in Italy, but rather trendy in many other countries. The biscuit market shows quite different patterns in different countries. (The extent to which different product types vary in their internationalization is discussed below.)

Local markets have different histories and structures

The development of particular product markets will have different histories in every country. They may be converging – usually because of the actions of the major multinationals – but their current situation may still vary widely. The brand share of even a leading global brand will vary across countries. There may, for example, be a very strong local competitor with an entrenched position. In such circumstances, goes the argument, a standardized strategy makes no sense.

Brands designed internationally are the lowest common denominator

If a company tries to take all these differences into account, it will end up with a compromise – something bland that offends no one but delights no one either. This seems a convincing argument, but it is not clear how many companies actually work that way. There must be some sensible compromise between taking all national preferences into account and ignoring them completely.

So far, then, it seems that some markets will respond to global brands, but some will remain stubbornly different. Are there any guidelines as to which category any particular market will fall into?

TYPES OF PRODUCT

It is impossible to generalize across the huge range of product markets. There are, however, some classifications that may help.

Culture-bound and culture-free

Products are said to be culture-bound if their use is intricately tied up with some aspect of the country's culture. Examples of products that are free of such associations are consumer electronics: we use a VCR in the same way regardless of our nationality and background.

Food, on the other hand, is thought to be intimately bound up with local culture, and indeed at first sight local markets for food products do vary hugely.

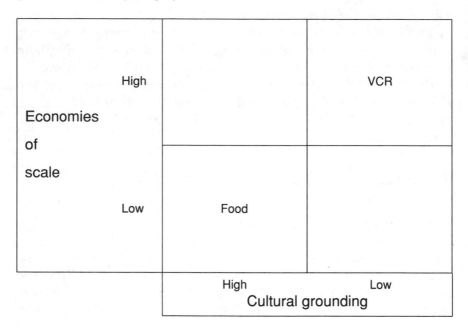

Figure 11.1   *Cultural grounding*

If the culture variable is combined with the availability of economies of scale, as in Figure 11.1, we see that food has low economies of scale and is culture-bound; it is therefore difficult to establish global food brands. VCRs, however, do enjoy economies of scale and are culture-free, so global brands are feasible.

Yet we must look at the evidence of Coca-Cola and McDonald's, both global food brands. We must also admit that in many countries, tastes are converging. In some socio-economic groups anyway, an international if not global menu is emerging. How far it has gone in a particular case will need to be determined by analysis. What is more difficult is to predict the dynamics of change: how quickly will convergence happen, and what effect will the activities of global brand marketers have?

Country of origin

We have been talking of global brands as if they were stateless. Perhaps some are, but for others their country of origin is significant.

For example, many famous global brands – Coke, McDonald's, Levi's, Marlboro – could only be American. Their 'American-ness' is an essential part of their appeal, and consumers are buying into a small piece of the American way of life. Likewise, luxury brands from France, both haute couture and drinks such as cognac and champagne, have a unique cachet that comes from their origin. Italian fashion brands such as Gucci would be less powerful if they came from England. German cars and industrial engineering products gain an additional value from their origin, as do Japanese consumer products such as electronics and cameras.

Some brands seem local, even if they are known to be international. Many people in Britain will have thought of Ford, Vauxhall or Hoover as British, though they are all American in origin or by takeover. This, say some, is the real challenge in the future for aspiring global brands: to have the authority of internationally acceptable brands while appearing local enough to be 'what we want here'.

WHY AIM TO BE GLOBAL?

Going global is always going to be expensive and difficult, but seems a prize worth aiming for. The reasons are various.

Must be global to survive

In some markets, as we have noted, global scale is a prerequisite for competing at all. In these arenas, such as pharmaceuticals and cars, economies of scale or scope are paramount in bringing costs down low enough or spreading high investment over large enough sales.

Clients are going global

For many service firms whose clients are international – advertising agencies, accountants, consultants – a global network is becoming a necessity. Any firm that wants to serve the biggest clients has been forced to set up local offices around the world, or to develop alliances with other firms to provide global reach.

Competition

The fact that competitors are going global is undoubtedly a spur. A firm may have to compete on a global scale, either to defend its domestic market against global competitors with scale advantages or to take advantage of new opportunities in new markets before competitors establish themselves.

Profit opportunities

If successful brands cannot be transferred rapidly to as many markets as possible, profit opportunities are foregone. Procter and Gamble found that, without central control, some successful brands were not introduced into major European markets for up to 12 years after their initial launch. The first mover advantage may also be lost, leaving the firm playing catch-up in too many important countries.

Strategically, these are all very real pressures. Firms risk being left behind, caught in a cycle of increasing threats and decreasing opportunities, facing only decline. But going global is also risky. How do they know they will succeed?

CONDITIONS FOR GLOBAL BRANDS

While there is no philosopher's stone that will guarantee to transform a humble local brand into a global giant, there are some fundamental requirements.

Sustainable competitive advantage

The firm must be absolutely clear that the brand has some differentiating advantage over the competition it is likely to meet in all its markets. Making this judgment demands a high degree of objectivity, and the commitment to maintain the advantage against imitation and attack.

Some economies of scale

The production cost function is not always linear, that is, costs do not necessarily fall steadily at the same rate as volume increases. There are likely to be steps, where costs rise steeply in the short term as production is raised to a new level. It must be clear that when the planned – or desired – level of international sales is reached, costs will be at a level that allows the company to compete with rivals.

A segment of viable size must exist in each target country

As we noted above, the segment does not have to be the same size everywhere, but it must be big enough to support the brand in enough markets.

The organization to implement globalization

Going from a multi-country to a global operation is impossible without radical changes in the organization, often wrenching ones. This is not a trivial problem. (This topic is dealt with in more detail in Chapter 13.)

HOW TO GO ABOUT IT

Assuming that the conditions listed have been met, is there a best way of developing a global brand? There is of course no magic formula, but evidence suggests that some approaches offer better chances of success than others do. There will always be counter-examples of successful brands that have followed different rules – and unfortunately failures that have apparently done everything right – but the following process looks sensible if not foolproof.

Develop the brand strategy in one place

The total shape of the strategy – essence, values, identity, point of difference, positioning, target segments, mix – must be developed. The drivers may be technological or market led, but the total brand must be thought through. This needs to be done with a concrete set of consumers in mind, and it seems to work best if it is done in one specific place. This does not mean that consumers in the global market place should be ignored; they must be kept in mind, but the lowest-common-denominator danger must be avoided.

Exactly where this should be will depend on the market. Frequently it is the company's home market, where it ought to have most knowledge and understanding. In a global, multi-product firm, that may not apply to all product fields, and there are two other criteria. The first is the location of the expertise: some country teams are better than others in certain product fields, and it makes sense to use that to advantage.

The second criterion is the location of the fiercest competition: this may seem unduly demanding, but there is a strong argument for making sure that the brand can win in the most difficult market. Competition is a powerful spur to creativity and invention, as well as to efficiency.

Check against all important target markets

The brand strategy must be checked for major negatives in the markets that will account for the majority of sales. The brand essence is the key; as we have seen, minor variations in the physical product need not detract from a consistent brand proposition. The only absolute barriers are those that cannot realistically be overcome in an acceptable time-scale, for example:

■ consumer taste that is likely to resist short-term change;
■ entrenched local opposition that will fight back strongly against the most determined attack;
■ government regulation that cannot be altered; and
■ lack of existing suitable distribution channels and the inability to create them.

Check elements of the marketing mix for major markets

All elements of the mix should be checked, again in the major markets, against the need for *unavoidable* adaptations. Only the brand essence and expression are fundamental, though the advertising strategy – which should state how the brand essence is to be communicated to the target audience – is intimately bound up with that. Truly global brands such as Gillette Sensor have a global advertising platform – 'The best a man can get.' On the argument rehearsed above, if the one best strategy has been developed, adaptations should be accepted only on the most compelling evidence.

Choose a suitable name

The name is central to many brands, but it is becoming ever more difficult to find suitable global names. If an ideal brand name is four letters long, then there are very few words left that are suitable, that is, that are:

■ pronounceable in all languages;
■ have no negative connotations in any language;
■ are memorable;
■ are at least not inconsistent with the brand essence.

There are many examples of names that turn out to have unfortunate meanings in some other language: the most printable is the Vauxhall/Opel 'Nova', which means 'does not go' in Spanish.

The days when George Eastman could invent 'Kodak' – a short, memorable, meaningless name – and take it all over the world, may be over. Words or even phrases that can be translated may be a better bet, though it is probably also worth trying an existing name even if at first sight it causes problems. Dove soap was launched in many countries, but the company was aware that the word in Italian means 'where' – which seemed hardly appropriate. But local managers felt that this was not a barrier, and it turned out not to be.

Select countries for launch and roll-out

Choosing which countries to launch or roll out a brand can be a complex process involving detailed market analysis of many countries. In other cases, the countries choose themselves, as only certain markets are big enough to generate high levels of sales. In Europe, brands aiming for a high share of the total market will have to be in Germany, France, Italy, the UK and Spain. Brands wanting to gain a significant share of a global market will have to be in the triad regions of North America, South Asia and Europe.

Many brands are launched first in their home market, and this clearly makes sense. An alternative is to launch in the country that led the brand's development, if that is different. The number and identity of other countries will depend on the nature of the product, the markets and competition. To maximize profits, the brand should be launched in as many countries as possible immediately. The Gillette Sensor was launched in 19 countries, for instance, and Procter and Gamble now make a habit of launching simultaneously in several markets.

Implementation and control of brands then become vital, and will depend on the organizational structure to be covered in Chapter 13.

12

Brand Planning

Brands need to be planned. This does not imply a huge, bureaucratic process involving lots of paper and little action. What it means is that brands have long lives (or should have), and they must be treated as such. The firm needs to think about the goals for each brand, and how to achieve those goals. The time-scale is years, not months – or rather, years for the long-term development *as well* as months for short-term action. As the first chapter stated, brands are so important that they should be the concern of top management, and it is at that level that the thinking must start.

CORPORATE STRATEGY AND BRANDS

Strong brands are already central to the survival of some companies, and are becoming so for others – whether they realize it yet or not. Branding must be at the centre of the board's corporate strategy. Observation suggests that this is true for only a few companies, that more firms pay lip service to the idea without actually doing much about it, and that many do not even see branding as a board-level concern. There are still too many short-sighted decisions being made that weaken brands: even the mighty Guinness admitted in 1996 that they had been guilty of short-termism in cutting advertising support for their brands, and that sales – and profits – worldwide had suffered as a result.

The top management must agree:

▓ the branding model they are using;
▓ the brand architecture for the company;
▓ the definition of brand essence for each brand.

The model must be defined and communicated throughout the company as a basic standard, otherwise there is no chance of widespread common understanding. A typical model is the Leo Burnett brand dimensions approach shown in Figure 1.1 in Chapter 1. There are many others; what is important is that the firm adopts one and applies it.

The architecture is the framework within which each brand fits. Decisions at corporate level include:

▓ *Company brand*: the role of the company, if any, in the branding process. Most large firms now have a corporate identity, with associated design of logos and house styles. The company as brand goes beyond that, as Chapter 10 argued. Times are changing, and even if a corporation has previously decided against company branding, it would do well to reconsider carefully in the light of global developments.
▓ *Umbrella and pillar brands*: for companies operating on a global or regional scale, and having many brands, some umbrella or pillar structure makes good sense. The challenges to brands discussed in Chapter 3 mean that individual brands will find life more difficult, and companies will find it increasingly hard to give them the support they need.
▓ *Global, regional, international and local brands*: the board must decide which brands can succeed at global level, as only the board can guarantee the commitment and support that this entails. Other brands must be assigned a role, whether regional, international (multi-domestic) or purely local.

The brand essence, defined using the brand model adopted (see Chapter 1), must also be agreed and promulgated. Having made these major decisions, the board must also ensure that they are communicated throughout the organisation. This is not always carried out thoroughly. Every staff member whose work makes any contribution to the delivery of a brand (and that means most people in the company, in my view) should be made and kept aware of these decisions and definitions.

INTERNAL COMMUNICATIONS AND BRAND CHARTERING

In recent years it has become increasingly clear that many of the problems experienced by brands have been the result not of a poor strategy but of poor implementation. In particular, there have been cases where market failures have been caused by inadequate internal communication. Especially in very large firms and firms operating in many countries, communication is complicated – but that only means that it is *more important*, not less.

Internal marketing is associated with service firms primarily: since a variety of staff deliver the brand – indeed to an extent *are* the brand – it is vital that they all understand in detail what the brand is. Internal marketing to all staff then becomes part of the branding process. But the same argument applies to product brands. As many people in the firm contribute to the delivery of the total product or service brand – and, as we have argued above, all brands contain large amounts of service – internal marketing is vital for *all brands*.

During the 1990s a new application called 'brand chartering' has been developed. Started by Kapferer (1992) but publicized particularly by Macrae (1996), brand chartering uses a series of workshops within a company to develop a consensus on a detailed definition of its brands that can be used by everyone in the company. Typical questions (see Macrae, 1996, p 10) that crop up in such workshops are:

▧ What leadership values would people – consumers, channel, company – really miss if this brand did not exist? Is there a common interpretation of the brand's essential meaning throughout the organization?

▧ Was this brand process ever in danger of being anchored too narrowly to a product or local platform? How did your company stop this happening?

▧ Is the brand's communications mix integrated and able to leverage changing media economies? Is it flexible for global and local marketing?

▧ Does the brand offer a world-class balance of quality and value?

▧ Do all the added-value departments of the organization

contribute to auditing this brand's opportunities and risks? Has the marketing department had to be reorganized to serve this brand globally and locally?

■ Is everyone agreed on this brand's claims to resources relative to other brands? Who is ultimately responsible for the brand's goals? Are measures of business performance well aligned with the specific goals of this brand?

■ What core competences does this brand represent? How does this fit with your overall foci for corporate competences?

■ Is the brand's platform linked to any other brands in the organization? Does your company use banner brands and product sub-brands?

■ What aspects of the brand process does the CEO sponsor?

■ Does your organization's culture promote a sensitive joy of change and a focused teamworking spirit? Would people be proud to be called a manifestation of your brand?

This approach, used in workshops involving a wide range of managers from throughout the organization, can produce a concise statement that can be widely promulgated. This, or some alternative method that produces similar results, is needed so that everyone who may contribute to the brand will have a common understanding. Local decisions that may appear trivial – but that may by themselves or in combination detract from the brand – can be taken in a way consistent with the brand's essence and values.

THE BRAND PLANNING PROCESS

In much of what follows, the angle seems to be most appropriate for a new brand. This is deliberate, as it serves two purposes. The first is that the development of new brands will be relevant to many readers. Secondly, *all* brands need regular reappraisal; approaching an established brand without preconceptions, with a blank sheet of paper, can give a valuable perspective. The more successful the brand, the more this is needed, as the greatest danger for thriving brands is complacency. The analysis may not need to be repeated in depth every year, but it does need to be updated. Assumptions and preconceptions should be challenged.

Market definition

This is not so straightforward as it may sound. Brand owners are apt to use very product-oriented market definitions, that is, ones based on their product and all direct competitors. This is hardly consumer oriented. The shopper does *not* enter the store saying:

34 SKUs please
6 in non-food category IV
2 countlines
3 ambient ready meals
2 hand-held wrapped impulse ice creams
... etc, etc

(Coopers & Lybrand, 1996)

In brand planning, you need to look at everything from the *consumer's* point of view, including the definition of the market. How do consumers see the competitors to your brand? When deciding whether and on what to spend their money, how do they see the alternatives? Some food companies now look at 'share of stomach' rather than mechanically defined share of market. Other firms are examining their performance in share of total spending. One way of defining the market is by asking consumers to state, for each brand bought, what they used it for and when. For each occasion, what else might you have used? For example, a packet of crisps might be eaten with a drink at a pub, as part of a packed lunch or as a snack at home. On each occasion, alternatives might include other savoury snacks – probably the manufacturer's market definition – or an apple, a biscuit, a chocolate bar or a piece of toast. Try new ways of looking, to see what new insights it may produce.

The other aspect to consider is the brand's served market. Is it serving the whole market, or just part? The measurement of brand share and the identification of competitors are both affected by the definition. The served market may be wider than the initial market as well as narrower. Honda has achieved world domination in small combustion engines by defining its market as all applications using such motors – from lawnmowers to generators. The brand strength can carry across these various applications, and indeed is self-reinforcing. Morgan, on the other hand, is not competing in the whole car market.

It may well be that you will need different market definitions for different purposes or time-scales. In the short term, you may want to measure your progress against your closest competitors'; in the long term, you may need to widen the definition. Brewers competing in the real ale market in Britain may usefully measure the success of their marketing efforts by looking at their share of real ale; but since that market segment is declining, they need to be aware of their total share of the overall beer market – and indeed of all drinks. A brand gaining share in a declining market may look very healthy, but its long-term future may be uncertain. Even a brand holding its own in a stable or growing segment may look deceptively strong if other segments or competing markets are growing faster.

Market analysis

This is the basic discipline of marketing. Analysis should cover the following areas.

Buyers and users

You need to know everything you can about your buyers and users – and other members of the DMU. The basic questions are: who, what, why, when, where?

The focus should be on the product in use. Too much brand research concentrates on attributes that are important to the manufacturer, but not necessarily to the user. A profound understanding of how people use the brand, where it fits into their lives, what problems are they using it to solve and what other products or services it is related to, is crucial to brand planning. Such understanding may be based at least partly on qualitative data, and should always be founded on personal experience. Even the most senior managers ought to be exposed to real consumers regularly.

Segments

What segments exist, if any? In mature or maturing markets, a sensitive grasp of the segments that either exist already or can be created is fundamental to successful branding. More difficult – but perhaps more important – is to foresee how the segmentation will develop over the years, and what new segments may be emerging. The ability to spot the growth of a segment of independent-minded young women led to the very successful launch – in a crowded market – of Charlie cologne. Renault saw the emergence of a niche for a new sort of family car, partly influenced by new laws on child safety; the Espace still leads its segment in Europe.

Competitors

Marketers today need a twin focus – on consumers and competitors. A single-minded focus on consumers may leave you open to an unexpected competitive move. Again, predicting future moves is vital, as is identifying possible new competitors; in the increasingly international business world, new competitors are certain to enter many markets. What are the Japanese, Koreans and Chinese planning?

Channels

If you use channels – and most do – they will be vitally important (see Chapter 7 above). Perhaps branders need trifocals, to see consumers, distributors and competitors at the same time.

Drivers

What are the forces driving the development of your market? How are they changing?

Critical success factors

What do you have to do right to succeed in this market?

The outputs from this analysis stage should be both quantitative and qualitative: market size, trend, shares; and a deep understanding of, and empathy with, buyers and users.

Brand analysis

Each brand should be defined using the company's adopted model. For a new brand, or for a reappraisal of an existing one, this process must involve market research as well as internal discussion.

Quantitative research can measure certain aspects of the brand, if not all. Some quantitative check on the qualitative output is useful – as unsupported small-scale research often produces rich and fascinating results – but may, because of the small sample, be totally unrepresentative.

On the other hand, market research can be over-used. Critics point out that relying on consumer research is merely reacting, not leading. All the competitors use the same methods and come up with similar results. The danger is that they then all design similar brands. Rather, it is the creativity and innovation of the firm that will produce real breakthroughs. Early stages must be qualitative, using unstructured discussions, projective techniques and any other aid available to a deeper understanding.

What research can do, however, is introduce a 'reality check' to see how consumers respond to a concept, or how they *really* view your brand as opposed to how you would like them to see it.

The exact output from the brand analysis will depend on the model adopted. It will contain something like the following:

1. *Brand essence and values.* The core meaning of the brand, expressed in a way that can be communicated internally and externally.
2. *Brand identity.* Users must be able to recognise a brand instantly. The design must give visual cues (the shape of the Coke bottle, McDonald's arch, Kellogg's big red K) and express the brand personality. Every communication medium *must be consistent and integrated.* In one case, the visual identity was designed in New York, and the advertising in London, with no contact between the two: the result was not happy.
3. *Place in architecture.* This should have been defined earlier, but must be stated here to check for inconsistencies and guide detailed planning.

Positioning

From its popularization in the 1970s, positioning has been an influential idea in branding. Many companies use a 'positioning statement' in their brand planning. The concept is that you position your brand in the mind of the consumer, relative to competitors and in a way that points out key differences. Obviously it is preferable if your position is unoccupied by other brands, and that it is one preferred by consumers. Volvo has always positioned itself as the car that is, above all, safe; BMW is the car with not only status but also sporting characteristics.

Critics of the positioning approach accuse it of contributing to the brand proliferation problem by encouraging brand managers to focus on their own brand to the exclusion of linked brands in the same family. A positioning statement may also be merely a re-statement of part of the brand definition.

The advantage of thinking about positioning at all is that it does make sure that you think about the way *consumers* see the brand and the placing of your brand in the consumers' mindspace *in relation to competitors.*

It can also be used, in theory at least, to re-position your competitors. In 1996, Audi advertising tried to re-position BMW as a car bought by bumptious yuppies. How successful this will be, as with all similar attempts, will depend on the realities of the products themselves and their buyers' views of them.

Aims and objectives

The aim of each brand should have been fixed by the board-level decisions discussed above. The position the brand is expected to fill in the future (five years from now? ten years?) should be set out to guide shorter-term planning.

The brand then needs quantitative objectives: sales, share, profit. It is here that conflict arises, and the pressures for short-term profit can wreak havoc on longer-term brand development plans. The reality is that brands do not have the luxury of being able to choose one or the other: they must meet both or many objectives. The challenge is to embrace and cope with multiple paradoxes:

■ profit and investment;
■ short and long term;
■ consumer and channel and competitor focus;
■ consistency and innovation; and
■ functionality and emotion.

As well as quantitative objectives, brands may have softer goals concerned with establishing the defined essence and personality in the minds of target consumers. The enduring aim is to *deliver superior consumer value.*

Brand plan

The brand plan should bring together all the elements into a coherent, focused whole.

Products, variants, sizes

What mix of products, in what assortment of variants – flavours, sizes, options or whatever – will meet the needs of the target market? The demands of operational efficiency, channel considerations and competition must be balanced.

Name

This issue was covered above. Within the constraints of the defined brand architecture, the goal is to find a name that expresses the brand essence, and is memorable and protectable. A further challenge is to combine a name that is narrow enough to be meaningful without limiting later extension.

Packaging

For some brands, the 'get-up' is a crucial part of the brand's identity; apart from the well-known Coca-Cola or Marlboro, there are Perrier, Lynx, Heinz and many others whose design gives instant recognition. In services, the coherence imposed by American Express on its diverse output was noted earlier as an example to emulate.

Price

Pricing is a strategic decision. It is a signal to the market of the quality/value positioning of the brand, and as such cannot be changed at will. It is also intimately linked with other elements of the mix.

Procter and Gamble have adopted a strategy of 'everyday low price' to their customers, cutting out expensive promotions that can disrupt production flows and confuse consumers. This, like many Procter and Gamble initiatives, will certainly be copied by many others.

An issue for fmcg branders is that price at the retail level is not under their control any more. The difficulties that upmarket perfume brands experienced when discounters tried to lower the price level dramatically was just an extreme example of the general situation. The final price can be influenced, and that will be easier when the manufacturer is working in partnership with its customers.

International pricing is also an issue, although many brand plans will be confined to a single market. Where the brand is sold in many countries, its price in each should reflect the overall pricing strategy, but be adapted to its local positioning. This provides opportunities to make higher margins in some countries, where competition is less or general price levels are higher. Variations in the retail price of cars in Europe have received considerable publicity, with Britain always seeming to be the most expensive – it is said to be known as 'Treasure Island' among car manufacturers. Sensible brand owners will try to balance the desire to increase margins with the need to offer their consumers value for money. Too great a discrepancy in pricing will only encourage parallel importers to source the brand from cheap countries to supply high-price markets. This causes problems with distributors in the target country, as well as with the brand manager! The situation may also be complicated by national or supra-national laws and regulations, as in the case of pharmaceuticals. Such situations can be dealt with only on a case by case basis.

Advertising and promotion

Consistent, solid advertising support is fundamental to successful brands, as many examples in this book have shown. The brand group may need to work hard to convince management – particularly the finance function – that this is worthwhile, but there is absolutely no doubt that, for most brands apart from retailers, it is essential. Even retailers may have to use advertising to change consumers' perceptions, restore a tarnished image, or re-position themselves. Marks & Spencer – famous for never lowering itself to advertise – suffered previously inconceivable sales declines in 1999, and 2000 saw it resorting to extensive advertising.

Promotion needs to be integrated into the total brand strategy. Well used, it can introduce excitement and keep the brand in the news. Used badly, it can weaken the brand.

Channel partners

We have covered the issue of powerful retailers. The plan must detail the strategy adopted to work *with* the distributors to achieve mutually profitable goals. Perhaps the brand plan and the annual review for each major customer should be developed concurrently, and with mutual consultation if different managers are involved. They should be saying more or less the same thing, but perhaps with a different emphasis.

Competitors

The plan should explicitly state what competitive actions and reactions are expected, and what the firm will do about them. Many plans omit this, and managers sometimes seem surprised by competitors' reactions. They must be thought about, and planned for.

Control and evaluation

Any plan must contain control measures, so that timely feedback will signal if results are off-course. The control measures should reflect the objectives the plan aims to achieve, such as sales, market share, new brand launches, increase in brand preference scores, level of customer approval ratings to be achieved, and so on. These must be easily measured, and the costs of doing so built into the budget.

As we said at the beginning of the chapter, planning does not need to be bureaucratic and cumbersome. In a large, complex organization, some formality is necessary so that co-ordination is possible. The main purpose is to ensure that the managers concerned *think through* what it is they are trying to accomplish, and to make sure that the plan is *consistent* and *coherent*.

MANAGING A PORTFOLIO OF BRANDS

Most companies have more than one brand; often they have more than one brand in a single product field. Each brand needs to be managed separately, but they also need to be managed *together* to avoid sub-optimization.

The ideal situation is that each brand takes as many sales as possible away from competitors, but takes as few as possible from your other brands. While the definition of brand architecture may have gone some way to delineating the area of operation for each brand, it may not have gone into enough detail to avoid cannibalization completely. If each brand appeals to a completely separate segment from all others, there is no problem. Unfortunately, segments are rarely watertight, and targeting is at best an inexact science.

Careful segmentation and positioning are the usual approach, and with constant refinement they can work well. Normally a firm with several brands in a product field will offer:

- a 'premium' brand, ie one that offers high quality and price;
- one or more 'flanker' brands, offering either a 'value' proposition (ie lower price for slightly lower quality) or a different set of benefits; and
- possibly a 'fighting brand' to compete with the own label.

The main brand should occupy the centre of the defined market, in the segment containing the most consumers. Other brands can then be used either to increase total market share – by appealing to other segments – or as blockers to prevent competitors taking over those positions. If the central position is already occupied by a very strong competitor, it may not make sense to attack it head on, but to use flanking brands as the main assault.

A more recent name for arranging the portfolio is 'category management'. This means developing a strategy for the category as a whole rather than for individual brands separately, and may include own label products packed for retailers. This has some appeal, and is often welcomed by the retailers themselves. This should make any company suspicious, and indeed one of the dangers of category management is that, in the short term, it is usually easier to maintain or increase sales by meeting retailers' demands than by concentrating on your main brands. There is a tendency for the own label, or brands designed especially for the retailer, to be given greater prominence than the manufacturer's brands. Unless this tendency is resisted, the brands will gradually decline. The retailer is also not being entirely altruistic in accepting the manufacturer's offer of help in category management; since it involves considerable data collection, analysis, planning and monitoring, it is useful to have someone on the supplier's payroll do it rather than attempting it on one's own.

13

Organizing for Branding

Strategies are developed by people in organizations. Organization is not peripheral to the task of branding, but central. Marketing organization structures are in a state of flux at present, as firms question classical forms and seek new solutions. At the same time, companies that had not previously adopted the old forms are taking up the structures being abandoned by others. It is a confusing time, when *The Economist* describes 'FMCG chieftains talk[ing] mistily about "evolution"'. In this chapter we will describe the traditional brand management structure, analyse the problems to which it has given rise, and discuss possible solutions.

THE BRAND MANAGER SYSTEM

This is what most people would recognize as the classical approach to running a brand-based organization developed in fmcg companies in the middle decades of the last century. The central idea was that each brand needs one person who concentrates on the totality of that brand, and who can co-ordinate all the functions that contribute to its delivery. In practice, that person has almost always been based in the marketing department, though in principle the functional background is less important than a holistic grasp of the various aspects of the brand. Each major brand would have its own brand manager, probably with several assistants. Minor brands might have just a single brand manager, or one manager might look after several small brands. In a large company, there would be a hierarchy of product group managers, marketing managers and a marketing director above the brand managers. The sales function was normally separate, reporting to a sales director.

Such an organizational device follows the logic of branding, and has clear advantages. These are summed up in a description of why General Motors in the United States are adopting the structure now (see Table 13.1).

Table 13.1 *Brand managers take the wheel at General Motors*

	The Old Way	Under Brand Management
Product Development	Engineers thought more about the competition than the customer	Brand managers work with engineers to ensure cars meet customer needs
Market Positioning	Similar models competed for the same customers	Each model must stake out its own territory
Marketing	Advertising, pricing and planning each handled by a different person	One person handles all aspects of marketing a single model
Product Image	Could change every model year	One consistent theme
Accountability	No individual responsible for a model's success	Brand manager's pay linked to model's success

Source: *Business Week*, 23 September 1996

The apparent success of brand managers in major companies led to the wholesale adoption of the structure in firms around the world – mainly in fmcg markets, but increasingly in other fields too. Yet by the late 1980s, the pioneers of the system were beginning to think that its drawbacks outweighed its advantages.

PROBLEMS WITH THE BRAND MANAGER SYSTEM

Many of the difficulties experienced by branding companies stemmed from the fact that brand managers tended to be young, ambitious people who stayed in one job for a rather short time – probably around two years at most. In that time, they had to make their mark, and therefore concentrated on actions that would produce immediate, noticeable results – changing the label, running promotions. The emphasis was on the short-term and tactical, at the expense of the strategic development of the brand.

As cost pressures began to bite in the 1980s and staff levels were reduced, the time available to deal with the thousand-and-one details became less and less. The growing power of retailers added new burdens to an already hard-pressed staff, and the strains began to show.

One study found several problems with the brand manager system. First, there is non-entrepreneurial bias, where passing the buck and an unwillingness to take risks prevail. There is also a tendency towards proliferation of brands, since both the managers themselves and their advertising agencies see more work and power for themselves with more brands. Moreover, complex, political power battles arise as each brand manager necessarily fights for resources for his or her brand. Again, this takes attention away from the real strategic issues of the brand. Finally, there is the value-destroying syndrome: the fast turnover of managers through the revolving doors of the career system means that experience and accumulated know-how are dissipated. Relationships between the people the brand manager is supposed to co-ordinate deteriorate, and teamwork suffers.

More generally, there have been other challenges to the marketing department.

CHALLENGES TO THE MARKETING FUNCTION

Cost and technology

Although these are separate in origin, they have together affected marketing organization. The pressure to reduce costs has hit every department and firm, and has been inexorable over the last decade; marketing departments are not exempt, and head counts are now lower in most companies than they were. Fewer people are just working a lot harder, but that may lead to the neglect of longer-term, strategic thinking because of the pressures of day-to-day problems. This has often been allied with new opportunities in technology, and has led most multinational firms to rationalize manufacturing at fewer sites. For those operating globally or even regionally, this has usually meant concentrating manufacturing in a few, large plants. Many factories have been closed, and often a whole region is now served by one or just a handful of plants, leaving more countries with no manufacturing capacity. This affects the marketing departments of the countries concerned, as decisions that they used to make may now be made elsewhere.

Globalization

The trend to international and global strategies described earlier has inevitably led to a reduction in the role and influence of the country marketing director and brand managers. If the strategy is developed for a region or the world, then the job of the marketing staff in many countries is limited to adaptations and implementation.

Retailer power

The complete change in the balance of power discussed in Chapter 7 has fundamentally altered the marketing task in companies. The need to develop a strategy towards customers in addition to consumers – and to co-ordinate the actions of sales, marketing, operations, computing, accounting and physical distribution – has thrown intolerable strain on existing organizations.

Marketing is not delivering

Perhaps as a result of these tensions, and perhaps because of marketing's own over-claiming, top management has begun to voice criticism of the marketing function. Surveys of chief executives and board members in the 1990s have shown that the marketing function is viewed more critically than any other. The classical, large, many-layered marketing department is 'often a millstone around an organization's neck', according to a McKinsey consultant.

POSSIBLE SOLUTIONS

As the opening remarks suggested, stating the problem is easier than finding a solution. Few believe that the right answer has yet been found – if indeed such a thing exists. The new organizational approaches described below attack some of the difficulties, but some problems remain.

Restructure globally

The companies implementing global or regional branding have necessarily had to adapt their management structure. The locus of brand ownership cannot be spread around every country, but must be concentrated. There are various ways of doing this, from the purely centralized to the dispersed.

In a centralized organization, a central brand group develops the strategy, which is then promulgated to the various countries for implementation. In a more dispersed structure, there may be a brand group in one country charged with *leading* the development process. The amount of consultation of colleagues in other countries varies between companies, but in any variant *some* consultation takes place – though probably with only the more important countries.

Whatever the exact structure, the role of the managers in subsidiary countries is obviously reduced. Depending on the policy adopted, they may be able to change some of the mix to meet local conditions, or they may have to fight to make any changes at all. In some firms, the post of marketing director has been abolished for individual countries, leaving only a marketing operations director – a significant move.

The problems that remain with, or are introduced by, the new structures could perhaps be foreseen.

Motivating country managers
Country managers were traditionally powerful figures – often

known, revealingly, as 'barons'. They were judged on their profit performance, and therefore wanted complete control over decisions that affected that performance. When important strategic decisions about brands are made elsewhere, they lose control and are not in a real sense responsible for the performance of their unit.

Motivating such strong-minded managers in a weakened role is difficult; indeed, many companies found that they had to remove some recalcitrant country managers before the new structure could be made to work. Those that are left have to learn to find motivation in being a member of an international team and contributing to strategy at a higher level.

Not invented here

We are all familiar with this syndrome – and probably have all succumbed to it at some time. Local managers will naturally resist a solution they see as imposed on them from afar, particularly when they have always argued for the uniqueness of their own situation. It is easy to imagine in such circumstances that mysterious difficulties arise in the implementation of beautiful strategies developed at the centre.

Growing the next generation

One benefit of the old system was that all brand managers learned through experience all the facets of the marketing job. They could start on a minor brand and gradually work their way up to larger ones, but they would throughout have to deal with the whole range of issues: briefing for and interpreting market research, dealing with advertising agencies and evaluating proposed campaigns, developing and running promotions, and so on. When many of these tasks are carried out in one location only, then very few young managers are being exposed to the developmental experience.

Category management

In this approach a team manages a complete category of brands and products as a whole, rather than as separate brands (see Chapter 7). It appears that some companies who claim to have adopted this approach have in fact just given a new name to an old practice, and are doing very little new. If it is carried through seriously, it can bring some advantages – especially to the relationship with retail customers. As we pointed out earlier, it also carries dangers for brands in that meeting customers' needs can take priority over those of consumers – and that is death to brands.

Business teams

The approach that seems most promising is the formation of business teams to market brands. The team should consist of a representative of each function that contributes to the brand's delivery. As has become clear, this includes not only marketing and sales, but also operations (manufacturing or the service equivalent), IT, accounting and physical distribution – and anyone else who is a part of the total effort. The need for co-ordination between these functions has always been clear. Now we perhaps understand better that to make them work together optimally, they must be in constant communication and see each other as team partners rather than rivals or as superior–subordinate.

Exactly how these teams operate may vary. In some cases they may be formalized in a permanent structure; in others they may form a floating project group, assembling and dissolving as needed. What is important is that individuals see themselves as members of the team, and totally responsible for the brand's success or failure.

Reallocate marketing tasks

We saw that brand managers had become ineffective for many reasons. One solution is to decide what are the *absolutely essential* tasks that the marketing people *must* carry out, and what could more sensibly be carried out by others. If, as this book argues, the central task is branding, then that is what the marketing people should concentrate on.

We should therefore expect the tasks to be allocated as follows.

Marketing:

■ brand development;
■ strategic principles;
■ market research;
■ advertising to support the brand.

Customer service:

▪ national account negotiation;
▪ relationship management;
▪ detailed pricing;
▪ customer support advertising;
▪ promotions (trade and consumer).

The result of this would be a smaller marketing team, but one which would need to be of the very highest quality. Developing and maintaining a successful brand is an extraordinarily demanding task. The marketing people would be freed from unnecessary and burdensome detail to concentrate on strategic brand development based on a profound understanding of consumers. Only then can they hope to meet the huge challenges facing them.

Each company needs to find a solution that matches its own unique situation and culture. Any solution will be less than perfect, and will need to be adapted as circumstances continue to change. Recognition of the dimensions of the problem is the first step to a successful conclusion.

14

E-commerce and Brands

The last five years of the 20th century saw one of the fastest and potentially most profound of all the changes our world has seen – the growth of the Internet and the World Wide Web. Jack Welch, CEO of General Electric, and probably the most admired businessman of his time, called it the most important development he had witnessed in his career. To cope with it, he called on his managers to 'destroy your business', so that they could rebuild a new model for the different world that was approaching. As a priority, he said, e-commerce ranked number one, two, three and four (*Business Week*, June 1999). The sad story of one famous brand illustrates the wrenching change that the new world can produce.

Encyclopaedia Britannica, the most famous encyclopaedia in English, started in 1768. Moving to America in the 1920s, it went from strength to strength: its comprehensive and authoritative content was allied with aggressive marketing to build what seemed an unassailable position. The peak was reached in 1990 but, since then, sales have fallen by over 80 per cent. *Encyclopaedia Britannica* had been overtaken by a new technology – the CD-ROM. Whereas a full set of *Britannica* cost the consumer at least US $1500, a CD-ROM rival cost only US $50, and in practice was increasingly bundled 'free' with a new PC. The new encyclopaedias were not serious competitors in breadth or quality of content, but to consumers they were apparently good enough.

Britannica dithered, at first refusing to treat the newcomers seriously. As sales continued to plummet, they then considered producing a CD-ROM version of their own – only to find that their 40 million words would not fit on to one disc, at least with illustrations and interactivity. When they produced a text-only version, the sales force revolted, as the CD-ROM could not produce anything like the US $500–600 commission they were used to on the printed volumes. The company bundled the disc with the printed set, and sold it separately for US $1000. Sales continued to fall, and the company itself was put up for sale. The price of the CD-ROM was reduced to US $125, but eventually, in 1999, the company recognized the inevitable, and put the whole content on the Web – free (Evans and Wurster, 1999; www.britannica.com).

There are several lessons here. The most frightening is that a 200-year-old brand, in a seemingly impregnable position, can be destroyed in just five years – and by a technically inferior product. The management lesson is that a strong company culture, developed over many years of success, may be a formidable barrier to rapid and decisive action when radical change demands it. The management knew – or certainly ought to have known, from their research and from years of experience – that the *Britannica* brand was about aspiration and parental guilt. Parents bought the encyclopaedia to do something for their children's education, but the average set was opened less than once a year. The product was grossly over-engineered for its actual use. When the world changed, parents could buy a PC for their children; the PC, its software, and the Web provided all the help the children needed, and the fact that Microsoft's CD-ROM encyclopaedia Encarta was part of the package removed the last vestige of need for *Britannica*.

The final lesson is that, even when managers recognize and respond to the changes, there may be little they can do. They are saddled with an obsolete business model – and with assets that once held real value, but are now worthless. The *Britannica* sales force was superbly effective in its day, but now had no purpose. The magnificent content remained, but no one wanted to pay for it. It is significant that Evans and Wurster, who tell this story in their enlightening *Blown to Bits: How the new economics of information transforms strategy*, thought that there was a happy ending. 'But there is hope,' they wrote. 'Britannica under its new management has produced a moderately successful CD-ROM product. It goes far beyond its competitors… The brand guarantees, as do few others, the seriousness and reliability of the content. The hope is to rise above the clutter and mediocrity that have proliferated in the early years of the Internet and build anew something of permanent value' (1999, p 7). As we know, even that model did not work, and it is unclear whether *Britannica* will survive in any form.

Not all industries and not all brands will suffer so dramatically. The problem is to look ahead and try to discern, however dimly, what the likely effects are. There are two mistakes in forecasting the future: to assume that *everything* will be different, and to assume that *nothing* will be. This chapter will examine what functions the Internet performs, and what the effects on brands and branding may be.

WHO WILL BUY OVER THE WEB?

Early users of the Web were often characterized as nerds or anoraks; they were certainly mainly young, male, white and college-educated. As the market has matured, this profile has changed; in the United States – and increasingly in Europe – more women are logging on, and the age spread has widened. At present, though, access is still highly skewed to the higher socio-economic groups. Any numbers quoted will necessarily be out of date, and the estimates of Internet use are notoriously imprecise, but in late 1999 it is probable that around 200 million people were online worldwide – over 100 million in the United States and Canada, and 47 million in Europe. Within Europe, one fifth of people have access to the Web on average, though this covers a wide range: from under 10 per cent in Portugal to almost 40 per cent in Scandinavia. The majority are still men – over 60 per cent – and British users had a household income of £40,000: twice the national average (all figures collected by Nua, 1999).

Figures for online purchasing are even more wide-ranging than those for users, but one estimate is that European sales in 1999 would reach US $288 billion; most of that must be business-to-business, as a survey of British consumer spending online was £2 billion (Nua, 1999). Over a quarter (27 per cent) of British Internet users have bought something online, and almost 50 per cent have used the Web to window shop and compare prices (CommerceNet/Nielsen, 1999). According to Nua, 56 per cent of British users bought a book online, and books continue to be the most popular purchase (1999). The general view is that most buying is of:

▪ books;
▪ computers and software;
▪ CDs and music;
▪ travel;
▪ financial services.

A huge range of goods is now available on the Internet, and new Internet businesses spring up every day. Most cannot survive, but it is impossible to tell which will be the lucky ones.

Evans and Wurster (1999) propose one model to assess the impact of the Web on a business. They distinguish between the economics of *information* and the economics of *things*. All businesses are a combination of the two, and each business offers a compromise: it is impossible to optimize the economics of information and that of things simultaneously. A retailer, for example, would maximize inventory to provide maximum information, but minimize it to lower the cost. As they point out, this explains why the retailing of some goods (eg books) is more vulnerable to the Internet revolution than that of others (eg food). For books, the value of the product is relatively high, inventory turn is low, and the premium on selection is high; the compromise suppresses value, and separating information from the physical product releases value. Amazon can offer a choice of millions of books, because it does not have to provide them on display in hundreds of shops around the country. Food retailers, on the other hand, work with products of low value and high inventory turn; beyond a threshold – say 30,000 SKUs – increased selection does not offer greater value to shoppers. Splitting the information from the product should not, in this analysis, release so much value – though one segment, who value their time very highly, may prefer to order over the Internet and pay for delivery.

Each business can analyse its value chain, and determine what are the relative importance of information and physical product, and what compromises have been made. In some industries –

retail banking springs to mind – bricks and mortar premises are an expensive way of delivering an information-based service, and they must feel vulnerable. Others, such as high-fashion clothing, would feel that much of the information inherent in the product is provided by the location, design and ambience of the shop itself (selection, interestingly, is increased by the clustering of rival fashion shops close together).

What each firm must also look at are their consumers. Every market will segment into those who are:

■ interested but unattractive;
■ uninterested and attractive; and
■ interested and attractive.

Unattractive customers will be those who buy very little, or are otherwise unprofitable to serve. Some people will remain impervious to the charms of the Internet, and will never shop that way. It remains to identify the interested and attractive group. At present, it is easy to describe them. They are:

■ young;
■ cash-rich, time-poor;
■ techno-literate; and
■ wired (ie have access to the Web).

These are the people who buy online, who sign up for Tesco Direct, and at whom Le-Shop aims its Internet grocery service in Switzerland. The question is, how much will that rather small group expand in *your* market?

The answer depends on how access and ease of use develop. Access is growing very fast in Europe, although actual uptake and use will continue to be held back by telephone charges – unless the telecoms suppliers change their tariffs. The spread of affordable 'fat pipes', providing the bandwidth that will enable fast download of sound and video, will also affect the attractiveness of the medium. Ease of use will be helped by interactive TV and by effective voice recognition. Much Internet access will migrate to handheld communication devices – the next generation of mobile phones – and in the medium term to cars, kiosks and kitchens.

There remains the question of how many people actually want to be interactive. Trials so far suggest strongly that most people, offered the chance, are happy to take control of their evening's TV viewing – but are not very interested beyond that. Internet banking, for example, is growing at only two per cent a year in the United States, and it has a very high 'churn rate' (ie customers leaving). If and when the process itself becomes automated – so that your refrigerator (or dustbin) records when you use food items, and automatically re-orders them – then the need for personal interaction may be bypassed – but that is still an idea for the future. No one has any idea whether such schemes will work or be economically viable, let alone whether consumers will accept them.

THE FUNCTIONS OF THE INTERNET

To explore further, let us look at the way the Internet functions: as a channel of communication, as a network and as a virtual company.

What is different about the Internet?

As a communications channel, the Internet is just another option for companies to use in reaching their customers. It is most similar to the telephone, in that it is instantaneous and two-way. Indeed, much of e-commerce is merely direct marketing with added hype. Consider a company such as Capital One, which offers financial services to tightly targeted segments.

When a customer contacts Capital One, his or her identity is established and file details are called up, including the last 20 transactions. Intelligent software calculates from these the probable nature of the query, and routes the call to the staff member best qualified to help – all this automatically, before the call is answered. This is a highly sophisticated service, but it is based on the telephone, not on the Internet.

Many Internet retailers, or 'e-tailers', will offer nothing more than this – and often rather less. In this sense, e-tailing will become just another aspect of direct marketing. What the Internet can add is interactivity, connectivity to other sites, comparison information and the potential to create a community. The telephone offers some interactivity, but it is limited. Interaction with a Web site can be a much richer, broader experience than a phone conversation.

Customers can do everything that the telephone conversation can offer, but much more: they can explore a huge range of Web pages, with pictures, sound and movement; download information; linger at what is interesting; return any number of times to previous pages; choose items to buy, and change the decision easily – and even configure the experience to their own preferences.

Interconnectivity offers further enhancements: from an outdoor clothing site, an Internet shopper can hop to check the weather in holiday destinations or the snow conditions in chosen resorts, and move on to a travel site to book a holiday before returning to the original site to order appropriate clothes and equipment.

Before (or indeed after) visiting an online shop, customers can use intelligent agents to compare prices and services – in theory at least. At present, while big claims are made for intelligent agents, or 'bots', their performance is not always impressive. One test found that: 'Not one of the shopping services came close to running up all the items I sought. And none offered the best prices' (Wildstrom, 1998). No doubt they will improve, and the possibility that consumers will be able to check a wide range of prices in seconds, from their desk – or wireless phone connection to the Web – is a prospect that some will find encouraging, others threatening. (The emergence of buying groups is discussed below.) At present, there is ample evidence that the price dispersion – between highest and lowest – on the Internet is just as high as between terrestrial shops. Moreover, online shoppers do not necessarily buy from the cheapest site: a well-known and trusted brand (eg Amazon) can charge a premium (*The Economist*, 1999).

Finally, perhaps the one area that truly distinguishes the Internet from other channels is the potential to form online communities. Such communities are a feature of the Internet landscape as a whole; the chance to join – and play a part in – a community seems to be a benefit that millions find attractive. Shoppers, too, can and do form communities in which they register their opinions and experiences of the product or service, without the intervention of the shop. Communities are more likely to form around high-involvement products (eg major durables) than low-involvement items (eg groceries). Where they do spring up, they will be something quite new, and it is not yet clear whether they will be an opportunity or a threat for the retailer and suppliers. In theory, any brand owner ought to welcome the chance to learn more about consumers' likes and dislikes, and the richness of unmediated communication will be fascinating. But such communities may also bring pressure – particularly on pricing – that companies may not find comfortable.

The other way that the Internet changes business models is the combination of richness and reach. Evans and Wurster (1999) point out that, traditionally, there is a trade-off between richness and reach. A personal sales call, for example, offers great richness, but poor reach; a TV advertisement, on the other hand, gives huge reach, but little richness. Sophisticated direct marketing techniques can add richness to a mailshot, but it is still limited by the medium's possibilities. The Internet, because of the size of the network and its infinite connectivity, can combine great richness with huge reach. While there will still be some compromises, companies such as Amazon can offer each of millions of customers a much richer experience than the most targeted mailshot.

What even Amazon cannot offer, though, is the physical and sensual experience of a real bookshop – which suggests the limitations of the medium. Internet shopping will not completely replace ordinary shops because, for many people, there are rewards such as the sight, feel and smell of goods – or the contact with other people – that the Internet cannot provide. Ironically, the very people who are the most likely to use the Internet may also be those who most want to get away from it. 'After staring at a screen all day, the last thing I want is to spend another hour shopping at one', may be the response of many.

THE EFFECTS ON BRANDING

The impending dominance of the Internet may have all sorts of effects on branding. It may:

■ transform marketing;
■ destroy existing retail models;
■ cause disintermediation;
■ modify existing models;
■ create new models; and
■ increase confusion.

Let us look at each in turn.

Transform marketing

The Internet is part of – and the result of – the broader revolution brought about by the whole set of technological changes in electronics, computing and telecommunications. Some think that the revolution will transform marketing. If change is constant but discontinuous and unexpected, then old models of strategy will no longer cope. According to this argument, the old model is 'make-and-sell'; even though – in enlightened firms – marketing guides what is made, it is still a top-down model. Where change is unpredictable, the new organization must 'sense-and-respond', becoming an adaptive enterprise (Haeckel, 1999).

In an illuminating metaphor, Alan Mitchell calls the old way the 'supertanker', and the new way, the 'cat'. Today's large corporation is a supertanker, with a pre-planned destination and route; it collects data on its position and on weather, tides, and the movements of other ships; it has a large database and sophisticated communications; it is very slow to change course if conditions alter suddenly. A cat, on the other hand, does not collect data on the mouse it is stalking: it waits, senses when the mouse moves, and pounces. If conditions alter suddenly, it can respond – even in mid-air. Tomorrow's markets will demand the responses of a cat, not a supertanker (Mitchell, 1999).

If these commentators are right, then large areas of business will indeed be transformed. Concentrating on our own field, we may see new entities emerge as 'demand aggregators', leading to the disintermediation of existing businesses. We have seen such processes before in financial services, where large companies now bypass previous intermediaries and go straight to the providers of finance. The large supermarket groups have taken over the role of wholesalers, causing many to go out of business. Indeed, we might regard supermarkets as demand aggregators themselves: instead of acting merely as channels through which dominant manufacturers distributed their brands, they decide what consumers want and commission manufacturers to supply them.

The Internet now allows new groups to aggregate demand. Buying co-operatives exist in many areas, but the Internet allows consumers to set up their own. In a well-known example, a woman in America was trying to get a better discount on a car, but the dealer was resisting. Eventually – through the Internet – she recruited 27 people who wanted the same model, and went back to the dealer. She got the discount – and indeed, bypassed the dealer to a higher level in the chain. If not too many consumers are willing to go to these lengths, then Web sites will do it for them. Mercata, with its PowerBuy, is a current example of such services (www.mercata.com). If they became widespread, they could transform some product fields – and their distribution chains.

As we noted above, there are also the effects of consumer communities and of price comparison agents. These will tend to make information more widely available – particularly information on prices. Bill Gates has argued that this will lead to 'frictionless capitalism', and that many businesses have relied on the friction for their profit margin. Another way of putting it is that information has been asymmetric: the supplier knows more than the buyer, and exploits that to charge a premium. Information – widely available over the Internet – will destroy that asymmetry, and restore some balance to the relationship.

Certainly, the one group that is sure to gain from the Internet is consumers. Some manufacturers hope that they may regain some of the power that they have lost to retailers (see below), but that seems wishful thinking. If greater consumer knowledge produces price pressure on retailers, they will surely transmit that to their suppliers. Only if manufacturers succeed in building a genuine new relationship with consumers will they win; we return to this later. Consumers have everything to gain, and nothing to lose.

Destroy existing retail models

The most lurid forecasts – that all supermarkets will be abandoned hulks around our cities, for example – are not credible. Some sectors will be hit hard, the travel and music businesses being prime examples. Others will be affected as some buying shifts to the Internet. The danger in such cases is not so much the *size* of the online segment as its *nature*. If a range of e-tailers manage to attract the most profitable customers in a sector – those who buy most, or tend to buy the products with the higher margins – then such cherry-picking will have a more than proportionate effect on the bricks-and-mortar retailers' profits.

For retailers, this poses a dilemma. If they react by starting their own Internet offer, to what extent will it interfere with their existing business? It is now clear that Internet business is completely different from the traditional form: it demands a different mindset, different skills and much faster reaction times – a whole new culture. How will the traditional retailer manage this switch? From a branding point of view, how will the Web site affect brand perceptions? For Tesco, this may not be a problem – as long as the Internet offer works well – but for Harrods, it is a real challenge. A comparative report rated Iceland's site above Harrods', which it described as 'surprisingly average for what is probably the most famous store in the world' (*Financial Times*, 1 December 1999). The response of Wal-Mart has been to say it will split off its Internet business and set it up with separate offices away from the Arkansas headquarters – as Procter and Gamble are doing. While 'clicks-and-mortar' operations (a combination of online shopping and actual shops) may be the best solution for many retailers, managing two very different cultures could be difficult.

Cause disintermediation

The most threatening models are Dell in direct sales of computers and Charles Schwab in share trading. Both exemplify the ability of online businesses to combine richness and reach, and the savings they gain by cutting out the retail stage of the chain mean that they can offer very competitive prices. As buyers in each market become more expert, they will feel more able to do without the help and personal contact they get from face-to-face retailers. A segment of personal shoppers will remain, but it may shrink to a minority.

Direct and indirect effects

Direct effects are easy to spot – though not necessarily to deal with. The fact that buyers can download music directly, or travellers book flights and hotels online, are direct effects – and already visible. Indirect effects could be the migration of classified advertising to the Web. If a substantial proportion of advertising for jobs, cars and houses, for example, transfers to the Internet – which is particularly suited to scanning and searching such material – the indirect effects on the profitability of newspapers could be profound. Many papers rely on classified advertising for a large part of their profit, and they have not had to work too hard for it in the past – especially when they had a local monopoly. Losing a chunk of that revenue could take them towards the vicious downward spiral of shrinking advertising–fewer editorial pages–fewer readers–shrinking advertising (Evans and Wurster, 1999).

Modify existing models

Many markets may see some modification of existing shopping patterns, without a total transformation. We have mentioned grocery, where the economics – at least in current models – do not offer huge benefits for Internet versions, and fashion, where the in-store shopping experience will remain a dominant attraction. Many other fields will be influenced by the Internet, but not transformed.

One variant is that some visionary retailers will use the Web to enhance the service they offer, and develop a competitive advantage. Home Depot in the United States, for example, allows trades people (small builders, etc) to access the Web site and get advice on a particular job; the software will then estimate the materials needed, assemble the order and dispatch it. Lively competitors will be constantly looking for imaginative ways of differentiating themselves.

Create new models

We noted the potential rise of buying groups earlier. The other new phenomenon is the auction and its cousin the 'reverse' auction. E-Bay is one of the Internet superstars, and now auctions millions of items of all kinds. In a reverse auction, the shopper enters a price he or she is willing to pay for an item – say an airfare from London to New York – and suppliers bid for the business.

It seems that only a certain sort of person will regularly buy in this way. Those who enjoy the thrill of the hunt, or who are willing to take risks, will take part. Others may do so occasionally, for certain types of goods – but not as a habit. Both are businesses that could not exist without the Internet. No doubt wholly new ideas will spring up in future.

Increase confusion

The Web is already a confusing place, and the number of sites continues to grow at an astonishing pace. Anyone who has used several search engines will know that they vary enormously in the number of sites they find when looking for a specific word or phrase. The Internet has an unparalleled richness, but the other side of the coin is total confusion. If a search for 'books' can produce a list of several thousand sites, then the temptation is to go straight to Amazon.co.uk, even if you know that their prices are not the lowest available.

In this confusion, consumers still want to trust their supplier, and so – paradoxically at first sight – the Internet brand becomes all-important. This is the reason that e-tailers are spending vast sums on advertising in conventional media (see below). Trusted brands – whether portals, navigators, agents, or e-tailers – will win; but the corollary is that many thousands of hopefuls will lose.

WHAT SHOULD EXISTING BRANDS DO?

The ways different brand owners have reacted to this new, frightening, confusing world range from the clear-sighted and proactive, through the cautiously experimental, to rabbit-in-the-headlights catatonic. How should you proceed? The only certainty is that there is no certainty: there are no general, one-size-fits-all answers. Wise firms will take stock, then act.

Analyse the situation

As marketing people, we should start with our consumers. Who are they, what do they want from us, what do they buy, when, how? All the information that should inform our marketing actions becomes even more important. We have to look at our customers from a different angle, or shine a different kind of light on them. Where does buying and using our brand fit into their lives? What are the problems with buying and using our brand, how could we – or someone else – make it easier, more enjoyable, richer? Is the shopping or buying experience enjoyable in itself, is it part of something enjoyable – or is it a chore? What are their attitudes to technology, and how are they changing? This is a tricky area, since we cannot just ask consumers. People do not know in advance how they will react to new technology.

It is already clear that access to the Web will be available not only through interactive TV (possibly voice-activated), but also hand-held devices (mobile phones, palm computers, and hybrids), and even the refrigerator and microwave oven. We also know that children growing up now are much more comfortable with computer technology than previous generations, and we can assume that this will stay with them. What we do not know is how interactive the mass of consumers will want to be. All that firms can do is watch – and be prepared.

Then we must think how our intermediaries may be affected. Using analytical ideas – such as the economics of information versus that of things, and richness and reach (Evans and Wurster, 1999) – we can try to work out how the structure of the industry value chain may change, and what the effect would be on our business. Such is the level of uncertainty that brainstorming and scenario analysis may be necessary to help cope with what otherwise can appear chaotic.

Decide broad strategy

If it is possible – and we must accept that, in some cases, it will be extremely difficult – we should decide on the broad strategy to adopt towards the Internet challenge. The basic responses include:

▓ carrying on as at present;
▓ dipping a toe in the water;
▓ developing customer service;
▓ developing new services;
▓ making a radical transformation;
▓ starting a new business.

Carry on as at present
If the analysis suggest that the changes in your market and in the structure of the industry will be incremental and slow, then it makes sense not to panic. Most companies have a Web site, and they can watch developments and react as and when they need to. To feel secure in this strategy, you also have to be very confident that no radical shocks can upset your course – whether from inside the industry or from outside.

Toe in the water

What many companies are doing now is allocating some resources to e-business, and seeing what happens. The Web site is probably interactive, and the firm will monitor customer reactions. You should also be monitoring what competitors are doing, and what is happening in different but similar markets. It is frightening that some 50 per cent of British company directors have received *no* briefing on the Internet: that suggests complacency (or fear) at the highest levels. The great majority of companies ought to be at least at this stage of development, and the top managers must lead.

Develop customer service

Using the Internet to enhance customer service is an obvious development. Best-known of the early ideas was FedEx's allowing customers to access their site to check on the exact whereabouts of their parcel. Similarly, many companies have developed extranets, and allow clients to access them for information or for transactions. For many, the extranets will replace EDI (electronic data interchange), which is much more expensive and restrictive. In business-to-business markets, this pattern is pervasive.

A choice that has to be made is whether or not to allow or encourage online purchasing. Much will depend on the nature of the product and the associated economics of transport and delivery: for small, low-ticket items like many fmcg brands, online buying is unlikely to be attractive. The other – and major – consideration is the relationship with existing intermediaries. Developing a new channel while maintaining the old one is always a tricky business, and some way has to be found to retain the support of current retailers. In this sense, the Internet does not present a new challenge, just a different and dramatic form of an old one.

The other possibility is to encourage the development of a community of customers. As we noted above, the Internet gives users a unique opportunity to exchange information and views. The company can actively participate in this, as long as it does not appear dominating or manipulative. Others could perhaps learn from the experience of companies in the computer industry, where user groups pre-date the Internet and have been very influential.

Develop new services
We described the Home Depot idea above, and this is typical of the way that the Internet provides new opportunities for differentiation. The radically different culture of most Internet businesses suggest that traditional firms may have to find new ways of stimulating 'out-of-the-box' thinking – new people, new organizational structures, new incentives.

Make a radical transformation
It takes a great deal of courage to set out on this path. Although Jack Welch called on his managers to destroy their businesses, few have done so. The difficulty – and the danger of being half-hearted – is shown by the experience of Barnes & Noble, the US booksellers. Starting some way behind amazon.com – who of course began with a clean sheet of paper – Barnes & Noble have spent millions on their Internet book operation, but are still a very poor second to Amazon. Perhaps only Charles Schwab has been radical, and has accepted that they have to completely cannibalize their old business to build their new online share-trading model. They have been notably successful, and even the mighty Merrill Lynch, having been slow to respond, is now playing catch-up.

Start a new business
Recognizing that the mindset and skills needed to run an Internet business are totally different from those required in normal mode, some companies are setting up a separate firm. Notably, Procter and Gamble have set up reflect.com as an independent entity in San Francisco to offer a personalized cosmetic service. This avoids the tensions and stresses of trying to run two different – and antipathetic – cultures within one company. It is suitable where it seems likely that the original business will continue in a reasonably healthy way, and can learn from the new operation without being disrupted by it.

BUILDING A BRAND ON THE WEB

For those who do develop a significant Web presence, the challenges of brand building are in some ways remarkably similar to those in normal markets. The first problem is that of creating awareness, and this is getting exponentially more difficult. In the early days of the Internet – when it was still the preserve of enthusiasts – a brand could be built by 'word-of-mouse'; as the Web became newsworthy, some start-ups benefited from widespread media comment. Later, banner advertising on search engines and what became portals worked – though at dramatically increasing cost. Now, start-ups that need to gain customers rapidly have to contemplate spending huge sums on advertising.

In late 1998, it was estimated that Internet companies were spending some US $200–250 million at an annual rate. A year later, the figure was US $7.5 *billion* (*Financial Times*, 1999). This rate of growth is unprecedented.

The problem the dot.coms face is that the stock market is making millionaires and billionaires overnight, but only for start-ups that demonstrate rapid growth in customer numbers. Profits seem irrelevant, but the ability to attract customers and keep them coming back is – almost literally – priceless. In the increasing clutter – an inadequate word for the situation on the Web today – making yourself heard is an expensive task. According to one expert, it is now impossible to build an Internet brand for less than US $100 million (Patrick Keane, quoted in *Financial Times*, 1999).

The advantage of being first, and early, may prove to be decisive for those firms that play their cards right. Those arriving later, such as Barnes & Noble, face an uphill struggle. And when you find competitors such as pets.com, petstore.com, petopia.com and pets-mart.com – all fighting for the same limited number of consumer dollars – then deep pockets and strong nerves are needed.

Yet, as we saw, consumer trust and brand awareness may be even more important on the Web than in earth-bound markets. When we do not even know for sure that a business exists, and have no way of checking – we can't look them up in the phone book, or go round to examine their premises – then trust becomes paramount; that is without the fear of giving away a credit card number, or having one's privacy invaded. If huge advertising budgets can build awareness, only superb service, consistently delivered, can build trust. Jeff Bezos, the founder of Amazon, says that it is pre-eminently a customer service company, and he has worked hard to make sure that the site is easy to use and the delivery service efficient. Even so, the experience of amazon.com in the end-1999 holiday season was instructive. Its sales rose dramatically, but it admitted that it had over-stocked to make sure that it could deliver gifts in time for Christmas; its losses also increased. Even with a brand name, the old retailing skills are still needed.

CONCLUSIONS

To quote one consultant involved in this new, strange world:

It's not easy, it's not cheap, and it's not optional.
(John Dickie, Insight Technology)

The Internet presents wholly new challenges, and managers will need to find new ways of meeting them. It is, above all, a top management responsibility. Companies in Europe have been slow to recognize this, perhaps because many senior managers have been personally technophobic. They may have a PC on their desk, but often it is only for show. Recently, there have been encouraging signs of change; but the change will have to be fast, and the new strategies determined, to catch up with our US rivals.

If your brand is Mars or Persil, the Internet will certainly change your business, but it may have little effect on your brand. You will use the Web to open up a new channel of communication with your consumers, and the task of integrating all your marketing communications will become that much more complicated. The companies most likely to see an impact on their brands *qua* brands are those in financial services and business-to-business, where the Internet may produce radical re-structuring.

As with any strategic issue, adapting to the new Internet age is a top management responsibility. The board cannot delegate this to the techies – nor to the marketing people alone. Top management must lead, and – as we have argued throughout this book – all functions must be involved in building a business fit for the twenty-first century.

References

Aaker, D A (1991) *Managing Brand Equity*, The Free Press, New York

Almquist, E L, Turvill, I H and Roberts, K J (1998) Combining economic and image analysis for breakthrough brand management, *Journal of Brand Management*, **5** (1), pp 272–82

Ambler, T (1995) Measures of brand equity, *Journal of Brand Management*, **2** (6), p 386

Ambler, T and Vakratsas, D (1995) Proceedings of the Peterhouse Seminar on how advertising works, *Centre for Marketing Working Paper 95–302*, London Business School, London

Ambler, T and Barwise, P (1998) The trouble with brand valuation, *Journal of Brand Management*, **5** (5), 367–77

Arnold, D (1993) *The Handbook of Brand Management*, FT/Pitman Publishing, London

Bullmore, J (1999) Private communication to the author

de Chernatony, L and McDonald, M H B (1992) *Creating Powerful Brands*, Butterworth Heinemann, Oxford de Chernatony, L and Riley, D F (1996) *Marketing Business*, November, p 55

CommerceNet/Nielsen (1999) www.q4.com/cnet.objects/templates /pr/pr271099.html

Coopers & Lybrand (1996) *The Future for the Food Store: Challenges and alternatives*, Coca-Cola Retailing Research Group – Europe

Corstjens, J (1990) *Strategic Advertising*, Heinemann, Oxford

Davidson, H (1997) *Even More Offensive Marketing*, Penguin, London

Doyle, P (1989) Strategic options, *The Brand in the Business: The strategic importance of brands*, The Economist Conference Unit, London

The Economist (1999) Frictions in cyberspace, November

Ehrenberg, A S C (1998) *Repeat Buying*, Charles Griffin, London

Evans, P and Wurster, T S (1999) *Blown to Bits: How the new economics of information transforms strategy*, Harvard Business School Press, Boston

Freeling, A (1994) *Winning the Right to Brand*, speech given on behalf of McKinsey consultants at the Marketing Forum on the 'Canberra'

Haeckel, S H (1999) *Adaptive Enterprise: Creating and leading sense-and-respond organizations*, Harvard Business School Press, Boston

Hamel, G and Prahalad, C K (1994) *Competing for the Future*, HBS Press, Harvard

Hankinson, G and Cowking, P (1993) *Branding in Action*, McGraw Hill, London

Jones, P H (1990) The double jeopardy of sales promotions, *Harvard Business Review*, **68** (5), pp 145–52

Jones, P H (1995) Advertising Accountability: Measuring advertising's effectiveness, *Commercial Communications*, **1** (2), European Commission

Kapferer, J N (1992) *Strategic Brand Management*, Kogan Page, London

King, S (1990) Brand-building in the 1990s, *Journal of Marketing Management*, **7**, pp 3–13

Macrae, C *et al* (1996) *The Brand Chartering Handbook*, EIU/Addison-Wesley, Harlow

Mitchell, A (1995) *Marketing Week*, 21 April

Mitchell, A (1999) *The Cat and the Supertanker*, speech given at Information Resources Open Day, London

Nua (1999) Nua Internet Surveys, www.nua.ie.

Randall, G (1993) *Principles of Marketing*, Routledge, London

Randall, G (1994) *Trade Marketing Strategies*, Butterworth Heinemann, Oxford

Robinson, B, Faris, S and Wind, Y (1967) *Industrial Buying and Creative Marketing*, Allyn and Bacon, Boston

Seth, A and Randall, G (1999) *The Grocers: The rise and rise of the supermarket chains*, Kogan Page, London

Srivastava, R K and Shocker, A D (1991) *Brand Equity: A perspective on its meaning and measurement*, Working Paper 91–124, Marketing Science Institute, Cambridge, MA

Vaughn, D (1986) How Advertising Works: A planning model revisited, *Journal of Advertising Research*, **26** (1), pp 57–66

Ward, R and Perrier, R (1998) Brand valuation: The times are a changing, *Journal of Brand Management*, **5** (4), 283–89

Weilbacher, W (1993) *Brand Marketing: Building winning brand strategies that deliver*, NTC, Chicago

Wildstrom (1998) *Business Week*, June

Further Reading

Bullmore, J (1998) *Behind the Scenes in Advertising*, 2nd edn, Admap Publications, Henley

Cowley, D ed (1991) *Understanding Brands*, Kogan Page, London

Kapferer, J N (1998) *Strategic Brand Management*, 2nd edn, Kogan Page, London

Keller, K L (1998) *Strategic Brand Management*, Prentice Hall, New Jersey

Marketing Business, published monthly by the Chartered Institute of Marketing, always contains news and commentary on branding issues, and is well worth reading.

The Journal of Brand Management sounds rather academic, but contains articles by practitioners too.

The group known as the World Class Branding Network (led by Chris Macrae) contributes to a World Wide Web site called MELNET devoted to branding. The address is: www.brad.ac.uk/branding/ and you can either browse, or join in and make your own contribution.

Index